THE PENNSYLVANIA GERMANS:
JESSE LEONARD ROSENBERGER'S SKETCH
OF
THEIR HISTORY AND LIFE

EDITED BY DON HEINRICH TOLZMAN

HERITAGE BOOKS
2008

HERITAGE BOOKS
AN IMPRINT OF HERITAGE BOOKS, INC.

Books, CDs, and more—Worldwide

For our listing of thousands of titles see our website
at
www.HeritageBooks.com

Published 2008 by
HERITAGE BOOKS, INC.
Publishing Division
100 Railroad Ave. #104
Westminster, Maryland 21157

International Standard Book Numbers
Paperbound: 978-0-7884-0971-4
Clothbound: 978-0-7884-7619-8

Editor's Introduction

Today, roughly 40% of the population of the state of Pennsylvania claims German heritage, thereby making the German element the largest ethnic component in the state. The Pennsylvania Germans, therefore, are not only of historical interest, but continue to play an important role to the present time.

They also occupy an important place in the annals of German-American history for many reasons, but primarily as a result of the fact that Pennsylvania became the focal point of German immigration and settlement in the colonial era.

Indeed, approximately one-half of the colonial German element resided in Pennsylvania. At the time of the American Revolution, the Pennsylvania Germans constituted a full one-third of the population of Pennsylvania.

The Pennsylvania Germans, hence, came to be the defining group in the foundational period of the German-American experience. Another important aspect about the Pennsylvania Germans is how they so successfully acclimated to America, and at the same time preserved their German heritage and identity.

Although Germans first came to America and landed at Jamestown, Virginia in 1608, and then later settled as well as New Netherlands, New Sweden, and elswhere, it was in Pennsylvania on the 6th of October 1683 that the first permanent all-German settlement was established in America at Germantown, now part of Philadelphia.

Thereafter, Germantown became the German-American center, and would remain so into the nineteenth century, and even later would still be an important German-American social, cultural, and political center.

The Pennsylvania Germans themselves have always been a fascinating topic to the general public, as well as to researchers. In completing my *German-Americana: A Bibliography*, I noted that in the section dealing with state histories of the German element that 21% of the registered publications dealt with the Pennsylvania Germans.[1]

It has been my goal to make a wide variety of works dealing with the German-American experience available and accessible again, especially as a result of the increased interest in the German heritage.

In so doing, the editor as selected a number of classics in the field of German-American history. The present work is no exception, as it is written by a Pennsylvania German, Jesse Leonard Rosenberger. [2] It is a work the reader will enjoy, as it provides an informative, but informal introductory history of the Pennsylvania Germans, and one which relates family history to that of the Pennsylvania Germans.

Rosenbergber most likely set out to write the history of his family, as the final chapter, "Gleanings from Old Records," deals with that topic. However, he also set out to write the history of the Pennsylvania Germans, including a discussion of their traditions, customs and life-style.

In this history, Rosenberger discusses German immigration, the process of leaving the old country, the difficulties and hardships encountered, pioneer life, religion and education, manners, customs, dress, proverbs and superstitions.

He also devotes a chapter dealing with the distinctiveness of the Mennonites as Pennsylvania Germans. The work also includes twenty-eight illustrations, which consist of photos taken by the author, as well as a detailed subject index.

This work is intended for the general public interested in the Pennsylvania Germans and their history, and can be considered as a basic introduction to the topic. Moreover, it might be considered as one of the best available introductory histories available on the Pennsylvania Germans.

For these reasons, it gives the editor great pleasure to make this work available. Those interested in further reading on the topic are referred to the notes, which contain references to sources pertaining to Pennsylvania German history.

Notes

1. Don Heinrich Tolzmann, *German-Americana: A Bibliography*. (rpt., Bowie, MD: Heritage Books, Inc., 1994). For references to works dealing with the Pennsylvania Germans, see pp. 53-61. For further references, see Don Heinrich Tolzmann, *Catalog of the German-Americana Collection, University of Cincinnati*. (München: K.G. Saur, 1990), Vol. 1,

pp. 204-226. For earlier works on the topic of Pennsylvania German history, see Emil Meynen, *Bibliography on German Settlements in Colonial North America, Especially on the Pennsylvania Germans and their Descendants, 1683-1933.* (Leipzig: Otto Harrassowitz, 1937).

2. This work originally appeared with a lengthier title as: *The Pennsylvania Germans: A Sketch of Their History and Life, of the Mennonites, and of Side Lights from the Rosenberger Family.* (Chicago: University of Chicago Press, 1923).

Don Heinrich Tolzmann
University of Cincinnati

JESSE ROSENBERGER, 1827–1909

Shoemaker, Farmer, Nurseryman, and Sometime (Baptist) Preacher

PREFACE

This volume is the outgrowth of an effort on the part of the author to get from the accounts that have been preserved of the Pennsylvania Germans in general and from various other sources such light as he could on the probable history and life of some of his forbears, who disdained to keep any records of themselves or chronicles of their times. By putting into this form the more important results of his study, with some of the matter brought down into 1923, he hopes that it may be useful to others.

General historical importance is attached to the Pennsylvania Germans not only because they contributed largely to the development and enrichment of their state, particularly agriculturally, but also because until within comparatively recent times they lived practically by themselves and tenaciously maintained, with local variations, the language, views, and customs which the German settlers in Pennsylvania brought from the

PREFACE

Old World. But most of these distinctive and interesting features are now rapidly being changed, or they have already been changed.

Practically all of the illustrations, with the exception of the frontispiece, are from photographs which were taken during the past year especially for them.

JESSE LEONARD ROSENBERGER

CHICAGO
October, 1923

CONTENTS

LIST OF ILLUSTRATIONS

LIST OF ILLUSTRATIONS

CHAPTER I

THE PENNSYLVANIA BACKGROUND

The general panoramic view in that portion of southeastern Pennsylvania that may be termed the original and distinctive home of the Pennsylvania Germans is an attractive one that is enhanced by the nature of the region, which is mainly a land of low hills and gently sloping valleys.

In the spring of the year, and again in the autumn, a person sees there farms that, for purposes of diversification and rotation of crops, have been subdivided into fields, which, when looked at together, have a certain pleasing harmony and contrast of form and color—one field, perhaps, being a green meadow; another field, brownish plowed ground; and a third, an area of yellowish stubble. Then, there are small orchards, considerable tracts of woodland, and, very frequently, particularly along the fences, occasional trees that in summer may afford a grateful shade for weary toilers, or—when in pastures—for cattle. But what possibly most attract the eyes of the observer are the clusters of farm buildings that are usually prominent in the picture, which latter may sometimes be made still more interesting by the inclusion in it of a rural church spire, of a small hamlet, or of a moderately pretentious village.

During the summer the scene is changed by the transformation of what earlier was bare ground into, first, luxuriant fields of green, and, later, of ripened grain—some of the fields being of wheat, some of corn, and some of other cereals or crops. At the same time, the trees, with their abundant foliage prevent monotony.

The landscape is also fine to look upon in winter, especially when everything is covered with snow, sparkling under a bright sunlight, the broad expanse of brilliant white being bounded by a somewhat shadowy circle of distant hills, and cross-marked by fences and trees. This scene is improved, too, by the groups of buildings which almost always include both a house and a barn of good dimensions, one of which two buildings may be white, and the other a bright red or a rich yellow, relieved in a measure by an adjacent orchard or a grove of dark trees that, dismantled, often permit of a better view of the buildings than is obtainable from a distance in the summer.

So far as the view thus described is the product of human labor, it is the product of the labor for approximately two centuries of successive generations of conscientious, sturdy, patient, hard-working, thrifty Pennsylvania Germans.

Two hundred years—or nearly that—ago, when Heinrich Rosenberger settled as a pioneer about 30 miles northwest of Philadelphia, in Indian Creek Valley in what is now Franconia Township, Montgomery County, what he saw was very different from the present scene. The hills and the valleys were there, and everywhere in the surrounding country, substantially as they are today, but they were then as yet untilled by man, were covered with a heavy forest of principally oak timber, and at best contained not more than a few log huts, which were widely separated from one another. The preceding human inhabitants of the region, some of whom might still be seen in some localities, were the Lenni-Lenape, or

Delaware Indians. Other denizens of the section were bears and wolves, deer, many species of smaller wild animals, wild turkeys, game and other birds of many kinds including at times great flocks of pigeons and crows.

One particular feature of that land of hills and valleys that appealed strongly to the first white settlers was that there flowed through some of the valleys large creeks, and through many of the other valleys picturesque little streams of sparkling water, the most of which are too small to be seen in a general outlook over the country. Along these creeks, or beside these little brooks, the early settlers built their log cabins, because they were thus assured of having plenty of water for domestic use and for the live stock which they looked forward to possessing. Nor were people in those days troubled with fears of such waterways becoming polluted and conveying the germs of typhoid fever, or forming places for breeding disease-spreading mosquitos, especially those carrying malaria.

The Germans were not of any appreciable number or influence among the first white settlers

SCENE AT THE VILLAGE OF SKIPPACK, WITH DAISIES IN THE FOREGROUND

SCENE ON INDIAN CREEK, NEAR HARLEYSVILLE

in what is now Pennsylvania, although there were a few Germans among the very early arrivals there. The discovery of the Delaware River is attributed to Henry Hudson, in 1609. He called it the "South River," in contradistinction to what he termed the "North River," which is now the Hudson. In 1623 the Dutch began settling in small numbers along a portion of the Delaware. They devoted themselves chiefly to trading with the Indians for beaver skins and other furs. What is now Pennsylvania was included in what they claimed as New Netherland. Commencing in 1638, the Swedes established colonies at several places, notably on the west side of the Delaware, and to a limited extent on the Schuylkill. They were largely farmers, who used the waterways as their highways for travel. To them the whole region was known as New Sweden. The English title dated ultimately from 1674. On March 4, 1681, the charter for the province of Pennsylvania was granted by Charles the Second to William Penn.

On October 28, 1682, Penn landed at Upland, which was then the capital. He changed its name to Chester; and subsequently Philadelphia, which was laid out in 1682, was made the capital of the province. The total white population of the province in 1681 was between two and three thousand persons, the most of whom were Englishmen and Swedes. During the next two or three years there were added considerable numbers of people from England, Ireland, and Wales, many of them being Friends or Quakers—in other words, of the same religious convictions as was Penn himself. In 1683 Penn stated that Philadelphia had about fourscore houses and cottages. In October, 1684, another man wrote that it was supposed there were then in the city four hundred houses, great and small. An estimate made with regard to the population of the province in 1684 indicated that it had been about doubled in three years.

The first historically important arrivals in Pennsylvania credited to the Germans were of Francis Daniel Pastorius in August, 1683, and of thirteen families (thirty-three persons) in October, 1683, these families being from Crefeld, near Holland, which undoubtedly accounted in one way or another for some of them having Dutch names. Pastorius came as the representative of what was designated the Frankfort Land Company, an association of persons in Frankfort, Germany, which purchased 25,000 acres of land and used it for speculative purposes. He was a man of good education, had a legal training, and drew legal papers and wrote letters for persons desiring such services; but for his main vocation he soon engaged in teaching school, which he continued for about twenty years.

Pastorius was decidedly of the opinion that it would be for the best interests of the Germans to settle by themselves, and not to be intermingled with the English, which he succeeded in inaugurating by obtaining, though not without difficulty, a warrant for 6,000 acres of land in one tract— 3,000 acres of it for the Crefelders and 3,000 acres for the Frankfort Land Company. The location of the tract was some distance from the Delaware because all the land along the river had been previously taken by others. On a part of the tract, Germantown was founded through a survey on October 24, 1683. In its early form and development it was much like some of the old villages which may still be seen, notably in Lancaster County, in that it was built mainly along the sides of one street. It eventually attained about 2 miles in length. It soon became important as a center both of industry and of influence among the Germans, in which latter respect it long maintained a supremacy. Thus began the separation of the German and the English settlers which was in the course of time to become very striking and was to contribute much toward the production of the Pennsylvania-German character.

In a letter which he wrote from Philadelphia on March 7, 1684, Pastorius described Germantown as being two hours distant from Philadelphia; that is, what is now a part of the latter city was then about 6 miles from the city. According to that letter, there was little open space to be found but everywhere only forests, in which there were massive oaks. On October 16, beautiful violets were found in the woods, and on the twenty-fifth there was discovered a wild grapevine that ran over a tree and had about four hundred clusters of grapes. The wild grapes, however, were rather small, and better for eating than for making wine from them. The walnuts found in the woods had such thick shells and small kernels that it was deemed scarcely worth the trouble of opening them. The chestnuts and the hazelnuts found were better. Of rattlesnakes there were more than were liked. But through the winter of 1683–84, which was a very cold one, no game could be found, although, according to some other accounts, game of various kinds was usually plentiful, in early years.

From that time on a gradually increasing number of Germans came to make their homes in Pennsylvania, until they amounted to about one-third of the total population of the province, which latter the first census gave as 434,373 in 1790. As three-fourths of these Germans were farmers who came with but little money, as time passed they went farther and farther from Philadelphia and from Germantown to get their land, seeking as much as possible locations where there were no settlers of other nationalities, and taking land that then was not much desired by others on account of its distance from Philadelphia, the labor required to clear it, and perhaps a misapprehension as to the quality of the soil. Thus it came about that the Germans were soon pushing their way northwesterly toward the Skippack and the Perkiomen creeks, in Montgomery County. Thence they went northward into Lehigh, eastward into Bucks, and westward into Berks, as well as began early to settle in Lancaster and other counties, as the counties are at present formed and named.

Nor was the settlement of the Germans by themselves so far as practicable their only form of segregation. Naturally people who came from the same locality in Germany, or who were related to one another, endeavored to settle as near together as circumstances permitted. But of greater general consequence was the extension of this tendency to the members of different religious denominations and sects, so that there were numerous distinct settlements of them, which helped very much toward the organization of churches and the establishment of schools.

Some of the reasons why the Germans came to America as they did in the eighteenth century, and what many of them suffered on the way, are explained in the next chapter.

A BIT OF SKIPPACK CREEK

PERKIOMEN CREEK AND BRIDGE BUILT IN 1798-00, AT COLLEGEVILLE

CHAPTER II

HARDSHIPS LEFT AND ENCOUNTERED

According to tradition, Heinrich Rosenberger came from Zweibrücken, in the Palatinate. It may be conjectured that he came prior to 1727, because, while he might have come through some other port, he probably came through that of Philadelphia, and, beginning in that year, records were kept of the arrivals at the port of Philadelphia, and his name does not appear in any of the lists. Why he came, as also why many other Germans came, can best be explained by referring to certain historical events. A consideration of these will also aid to a better understanding of the general type of the Pennsylvania Germans.

Heavy toll was taken of the people of Germany by the Thirty Years' War which ended in 1648. Some authorities compute that through it at least two-thirds of the population perished, and that more than two-thirds of the domestic animals and other forms of personal property were either consumed or destroyed. After that there continued for years an application of the torch and a pillaging by bands of soldiers from the troops which were still quartered on the inhabitants of various localities.

The next generation had the War of the Grand Alliance, and not long afterward occurred the War of the Spanish Succession, which lasted until 1713; and from these wars the Palatinate in particular suffered, as it had from the Thirty Years' War.

The peasants or farmers who survived that period had little, or nothing left. As a rule, the most of their furniture and their implements, their live stock and their poultry had either been taken from them or wantonly destroyed, and their houses had been burned, or razed. Consequently thereafter they found themselves with poor shelter, few furnishings, scanty rations, and not much besides their hands with which to do anything. They might be called the owners of their usually small farms; but the majority of them had to the lands only limited titles, to which were attached many burdensome conditions and restrictions, while at any time they might be compelled to sell their interest in their land. Three whole days, or six half-days, each week, with his team, if he had one, must each farmer work for the landlord to whom his obligations ran. The landlord must be given a share of all the grains, fruits, and vegetables raised. He must be offered first whatever the farmer had to sell, and whatever the farmer wanted to buy must be bought from him, if he had it to sell. He had a supervision over the marriage of the farmer's children, and a fine had to be paid to him for every marriage, while to each of his own children when they got married presents had to be given. Moreover, he had a right to call into his service for several years any of the farmer's children who were able to work. Nor could they enter service elsewhere without first purchasing a license from him; and he took special pains to prevent their flight. His permission must also be obtained for the farmer to change his vocation, or to be away overnight. In addition, there was taxation by the state, and the farmer and his sons were subject to military service.

Both the nobility and the artisan class treated the farmers or peasantry as being at the bottom of the social scale, and they showed such a determination to keep them there that neither the peasants nor their children had any appreciable chance to change their lot or to improve their condition. In the sphere into which they were born they must expect to live and die. In short, life for them was but a round of hard, monotonous toil, the most of the fruits of which went to the support of the state and the nobility.

Then there was always more or less religious persecution. The Palatinate at times furnished an asylum for the religiously oppressed, and at other times was a place of oppression and persecution. Whichever of these characters it at any time manifested depended on the character of the reigning elector, whether he was tolerant or not, and to what church he adhered. Thus, along in the seventeenth century, one elector belonged to the Reformed church, his successor to the Lutheran church, and the next one to the Catholic church, and each one of them believed in the common doctrine of his day that the religion of the ruler should be that of his people, which he endeavored to enforce.

Out of these conditions there quite naturally arose a desire that grew into a purpose on the part of many of these sufferers from ill fortune and oppression to seek in the New World the peace and the independence which had been denied to them in the fatherland, and which they yearned after for themselves as well as coveted for their children, with the opportunity in addition for the latter to better their material and social conditions. These aspirations and determination were in some instances created, and in others developed, by the various forms of advertising done by Penn to secure good settlers for his province; by the activities of subordinate colonizers, exploiters, and shipowners; by agents; by widely distributed pamphlets; by reports from one person to another; and by letters from relatives or friends who had already gone to Pennsylvania and were pleased therewith.

Large numbers of the Palatines in particular were moved to seek this land of promise. In fact, so numerous were they that for many years all the

Germans who arrived at the port of Philadelphia were designated Palatines, as if they all came from the Palatinate.

Many of the Germans, especially those who came in the earlier days to Pennsylvania, while they were in no sense wealthy, had sufficient money to pay their passage and have enough left with which to buy land for a farm and to get a fair start. But for the most of those who, in order to better their worldly condition, or to escape from oppression and persecution, wanted to come to America, it was a difficult thing to do. They did not have, as they could not under the circumstances have been expected to have, enough money for such an undertaking. Besides, various obstacles were placed in their way by those who wanted to keep them where they were to till the soil and to do other kinds of work, to pay the different forms of tribute and taxes, and to render military service.

Once these difficulties were overcome, there remained the hardships of the journey, which were increased with the multiplication of the number of persons seeking to make it far beyond the accommodations for it. The voyage across the Atlantic was generally very trying because it had to be made in comparatively small, slow-sailing ships, which were unconscionably over-crowded, and often inadequately provided with food and water; while many captains and avaricious ship-owners not only were indifferent to the comfort of their passengers but were disregardful of their lives.

Pastorius declared that the ship in which he came could be likened to nothing but Noah's Ark, on account of the differences in the ages, religions, occupations, and social standing of the passengers, as well as their division into clean (reasonably) and unclean. He described the fare as being very bad. Every ten persons received each week three pounds of butter; daily, four cans of beer and two cans of water; at noon, every day in the week, meat; and three days at noon, fish, which the passengers had to dress with their own butter; while every day they had to keep from their dinner enough for their supper. But the worst of it all was that both the meat and the fish were so salty and smelled so strong that they were not palatable.

Gottlieb Mittelberger, a church organist and schoolmaster, who came here in 1750 and returned to Germany four years later, said, in his *Journey to Pennsylvania*, that the journey from the Palatinate to Pennsylvania required fully half a year, amid such hardships as no one could adequately describe. One reason was that the trip down the Rhein from Heilbronn to Holland took from four to six weeks because there were thirty-six custom-houses to be passed, at all of which the boats (barges) had to be examined, which examinations were made when it suited the convenience of the officials to make them. In Holland there was a further detention of the people for five or six weeks. During these delays many persons had to spend nearly all the money and to consume the most of the provisions which they had taken with them. Both in Rotterdam and in Amsterdam, the usual seaports for re-embarkation, the passengers were packed densely in the ships, like herrings, it might be said, one person receiving a place scarcely 2 feet wide and 6 feet long for his bed. If the winds were contrary, it might require, instead of eight days or less, from two to four weeks to go from Holland to Cowes, on the Isle of Wight, where the ship might be detained a week or two in order to complete her cargo. From there the voyage to Philadelphia might require from seven to twelve weeks. Not only was the stench on shipboard almost unbearable, but there were many kinds of sickness, with miserable deaths, owing partly to the old and sharply salted food, and partly to the foul, impure water furnished. There was suffering from hunger, thirst, heat, cold, dampness, and anxiety.

Another very common, but almost tragic, hardship which many passengers experienced was in having their chests, into which they had put practically everything that they had to bring with them, broken into and plundered of a part or of all their contents, such as surplus clothing, linens, books, keepsakes, small utensils, and money. Other passengers suffered from having their chests sent on different ships from the ones on which they came, which at best caused them much inconvenience, while frequently the chests were never seen again by their owners, or only after they had been rifled of what was most valuable in them.

Then there was a large class of Germans who must have suffered their full share in the fatherland, and on the whole more than any other class in reaching Pennsylvania, but who had years of servitude yet to undergo before they could call themselves their own masters. They have generally been called "redemptioners." In one way or another, perhaps by selling their few belongings, they managed to reach a seaport, sometimes with their families, but had no money to go farther. In order to cross the ocean, they contracted with the shipmasters for credit for their passage until they reached Philadelphia, with the provision that if the amount was not then paid by them, anyone who wished to do so might pay it, and they would work for him long enough to repay him, which usually took from three to five years. This was an application of a method which had been used largely for English and Irish servants who contracted, in consideration among other things of receiving specified advances, generally including the prepayment of their passage, to go to America to work for designated periods for the individuals who personally or through their agents were the other parties to those contracts. Both those servants and the redemptioners were by their contracts and officially termed "indentured servants." Many, too, besides Germans came as redemptioners.

Unfortunately, however, it was not long before a regular traffic in German redemptioners was being conducted, often with deception and shameful ill-treatment. Agents of shipowners and captains went through the country and by gross misrepresentations induced people to go as redemptioners. Sometimes persons were even enticed on to vessels to be taken as redemptioners. After that their treatment on shipboard was almost invariably without any regard for their comfort or well-being. Nor was any consideration given as to the kind of persons to whom they were finally disposed, while members of families were often separated. It has been said also that there were men, called "soul-drivers," who, as it were, bought redemptioners in considerable numbers from captains of ships and took them through the country, reselling them to the farmers. Again, redemptioners were sometimes advertised for sale, as if they were chattels.

But it was not all like that. For large numbers of persons, this system of giving credit for the passage with a chance to pay for it afterward in work furnished the only means by which they could ever reach America, and it was of unmistakable advantage to them. Many of them got good masters and good homes, with a chance to get acquainted with their new environment and to prepare well for what they wanted subsequently to do.

An act passed in 1700 provided that every servant who should faithfully serve four years or more should at the expiration of his time have two complete suits of clothes, one of which should be new, and that he should be furnished with a new ax, a grubbing hoe, and a weeding hoe. In some cases contracts were made that at the end of his service a man should receive a horse; or, at the end of her service, a woman should be given a cow, or a spinning wheel. Children who came as redemptioners must work until they became of age, but with the provision sometimes made that they should be taught a trade, or so that they could read the German Bible, or to read English, or to read and write, and perhaps to cipher.

In several instances a redemptioner was procured to render services as a schoolmaster, or even as a minister. Furthermore, as a class, the German redemptioners are to be credited with becoming good citizens.

How the early German settlers as a class met the hardships or conditions which confronted them after they reached Pennsylvania—or what they then did and how they then lived—a brief review will show accorded with their developed character and their fortitude under prior adverse circumstances.

CHAPTER III

WITH THE PIONEERS

The life of a pioneer is of necessity one of privation. Moreover, the hardships attending it are generally increased by the fact that the most of those who enter on it are persons of limited means who are for that reason unable to provide as many things for themselves as they might otherwise have for their comfort and to aid them in their work. That was the case with the great majority of the early German settlers in Pennsylvania. But the narrow and almost comfortless life of toil which they had up to that time led prepared them in a manner for what was ahead of them when they set out with scant resources to make for themselves homes in the forests of a new country. Such peculiarities as their disposition to keep by themselves, their restricted ambitions, and their habits of industry and thrift also tended to fit them for the task before them, and to make of them afterward exceptionally good farmers; so

TYPES OF AMISH MEN, WOMEN, AND CHILDREN OF LANCASTER COUNTY

that with singleness of purpose and unsparing of themselves they brought their land under cultivation and thereafter labored to make it produce as much as possible.

Various makeshifts for temporary shelter while they were getting their allotments of land and erecting huts thereon had to be resorted to by those who came in very early times. During the warm months some camped under large overhanging trees. Others made huts or shelters of poles and the branches and leafage of trees. For several years after Philadelphia was laid out, what have often been called "caves," although the most of them were more like huts, were dug or built either in the side or at the top of the moderately high and steep bank of the Delaware River, near the wharf where the ships were accustomed to land their passengers. Some of these shelters may have been little more than large holes dug into the bank, which led to their being called "caves." But the most common form of construction appears to have been to make an excavation about 3 feet deep and of the desired length and width, and to build on the walls of that excavation extensions of those walls upward to the necessary height, using therefor either sods or earth and the branches and foliage of trees. The roof was made either of poles or of the branches of trees, on which were placed first bark or brush and then a layer of sod or earth. Chimneys were built of stones and a mixture of clay and grass, or of such mixture only. Some of these shelters served several tenants in succession, but some of them came to be put to uses which finally led to the issuance of an order that all must be vacated so that they might be demolished.

Pastorius described a house that he built as being one-half under the earth, and one-half above it, with a window made of oiled paper. He said that the house was 30 feet long, and 15 broad; but, when the people from Crefeld were lodging with him, it was capable of accommodating twenty persons. He said further that, besides building this house, he had—on the Delaware— dug a cellar 20 feet long, 12 wide, and 7 deep. Probably it was the house that was referred to when it was said that on October 25, 1683, there was a meeting in his "cave" for the purpose of drawing lots for choices of location in Germantown, although what he called a cellar was more like a cave than was his house.

After the division and assignment of land in Germantown those who desired to winter there had no time to lose in preparing for it. Something like the caves or sod houses along the Delaware were built from the materials at hand. That nothing better could be done was shown by the kind of house that Pastorius had to be content with in Philadelphia. But when he wrote his letter, in March, 1684, he exulted over the fact that forty-two people, distributed in twelve homes, were at that date living in Germantown.

Then came log cabins. Many of these were small and hastily built to be used for a year or two only, or until larger and better log houses could be built that would be very comfortable and perhaps serve for a generation or more. The timber from which to build them was to be found on every farm and cost nothing beyond the labor of cutting down the trees and preparing from them the necessary logs and boards, whereas the trees had to be chopped down to clear the land.

For the walls of the better houses the logs were hewed on at least three sides so that when laid one above another they would come close together and on the inside of the houses the walls, which were not plastered, would be fairly smooth. At the corners of the houses the ends of the logs were hewed and notched so that they fitted and held like dovetailing. The erection of the walls, after the logs had been prepared and brought where they were to be used, was generally done with the assistance of neighbors, in bees, or, as they were commonly called, "frolics." The interstices between the logs were stopped with clay. Roofs were constructed of poles and above them a thatch of grass, reeds, or, when it was to be had, straw. A little later, overlapped boards, and then rude shingles, were used, instead of thatching. At first the bare ground was sometimes utilized for floors, but floors were more often made of split or hewed logs, and afterward of boards. Chimneys were built of stones, the cracks between them being closed with clay, or with clay and grass mixed. The location of the chimney was usually against one end of a house, on the outside. Small windows were made by cutting holes of the desired size through the walls, and, when necessary, covering these openings with oiled paper or oiled skins until window glass was obtained. Window-panes were small and were usually set in leaden frames. Doors consisted of two parts, an upper and a lower one, each with its own hinges and fastenings, which made it convenient to use the upper halves of the doors as large, open windows.

The log house built by Heinrich Rosenberger, which was used for almost eighty years, first by him and then by his son Heinrich, was a typical log house of the better kind in early days, in that it was a story-and-a-half in height, or had side walls a little more than one story high, and rising from them a steep roof, so that the attic, having windows in the gables, made a usable room. In some houses of that kind the first story was divided into two rooms; in other cases it was left all in one room. The attic was often reached by a ladder that was easily made and that occupied little space. In other houses there were stairs, which were in some instances made by hewing out steps across a log of large diameter that would be erected with the proper slant between the floors.

When more room was wanted than a house of the foregoing description furnished, it was ordinarily obtained by building against one side of the house a log addition with a roof connecting with the roof on that side of the house, but with the roof of the addition having much less slope than that of the house. The addition was generally used as a kitchen, or as a kitchen and dining-room combined.

Almost every house had under it a cellar, which was little or nothing more than an excavation of the size desired.

An open fireplace served for purposes of cooking, heating in cold weather, and to a great extent for lighting in the evening. It was built in a hole cut for it through the wall opposite the lower part of the chimney. Its bottom, sides, and top were constructed of flat stones, while its back was a part of the chimney. All cracks in it were filled with clay.

As the people had no matches, they seldom intentionally permitted their fires to go out, but covered them at night with ashes so that embers might be found in the morning with which to start them again. When fires accidentally went out, new ones had to be started by striking a piece of flint with a piece of steel in such a way as to make a spark that would ignite a bit of tinder; or gunpowder might be placed in the pan of the lock of a flint-lock musket and flashed against some tow. It was also a common practice, when there were neighbors near enough, to go with a small iron pot to the house of a neighbor to get a few live coals with which to start a fire. When other light than that furnished by the fireplace was wanted it was obtained from candles made by repeatedly dipping wicks in melted tallow, which led to the candles often being called "dips," or "tallow dips."

The furnishings of a log house were at first few and simple. The furniture ordinarily consisted of a table, benches and stools for seats, possibly a corner cupboard, and a bedstead—all of them homemade. But if the house was one with an attic, the place for sleeping might be upstairs, in beds laid on the floor, each bed consisting of nothing more than two ticks filled with such material as was to be had, ranging from hay to feathers, according to circumstances, one tick being used to sleep on, and the other one, which was usually lighter, for covering. Wooden pegs, on which to hang clothing, were driven into the walls; and shelves, to hold the few books, dishes, and various other articles, were at convenient places attached to the walls. Linens and things of that character were kept in the family chest, which was soon supplemented with something like a plain dresser. The cooking utensils were few and primitive, such as could be used with an open fireplace, the main ones being two or three iron pots. Likewise, the tableware was limited to a few pewter dishes and wooden platters, and to some knives, forks, and spoons.

Those who had the means with which to do it, could purchase, in Philadelphia or in some of the older settlements of the province, horses, oxen, cows, hogs, sheep, and poultry, derived from some which the Swedes or the English had brought in from New England or possibly from nearer colonies. But most of the German pioneers had to be content to stock their farms gradually. Their first teams were generally of oxen; and not all got those immediately.

But as soon as a man had a house in which he and his family could live, he must, whether he had a team or not, enter upon the arduous task of clearing his land for cultivation, especially enough of it to begin raising as soon as possible the grain, vegetables, and flax needed for food and clothing. All the tools that a man had to have to do this work were an ax and a grubbing hoe. He began by grubbing up the underbrush and the saplings, which were gathered into piles and when dry enough were burned. He then chopped down the trees and converted as much of their trunks as he desired into fence rails and firewood. All of the refuse and the tops of the trees that were simply cut down and no part of them used were subsequently burned. After the logs remaining on the ground were generally brought together, piled, and burned by a "logging bee" composed of neighbors who termed it a "frolic." That is the way in which a German usually prepared his land for the plow.

Another method, which was generally followed by other settlers, was not to chop down any large trees, but to girdle them by cutting out around each one a band a few inches wide and as deep as the bark, or a little deeper, which would kill the trees. In a year or two the dead limbs would begin to fall, and eventually the trees, one by one. That saved some labor at first, but the branches that fell had to be collected from time to time, and burned; and so did the trees themselves, after a number of years. Besides, it left such unsightly fields that travelers remarked on the much better appearance of those cleared by the Germans. The looks of the fields where the trees were girdled and left standing were made worse, too, many times, by setting the trees afire, after they had become dry, and burning off their tops and the outside of their trunks.

Breaking the land by the first plowing, after it was cleared, was a very difficult matter because the trees extended far in all directions and the roots of the smaller vegetation intertwined, forming a close, tough network hard to be torn apart by the wooden plows with which it had to be done. If a man did not himself own a team with which to do this work, he had to hire one of some neighbor, and oxen were better for the work than were horses. Harrows with wooden teeth were used for pulverizing and smoothing plowed ground.

Fields had to be fenced for the protection of crops because cattle and hogs were universally allowed to run at large. The fences built were what have come to be known either as "worm" fences or as "snake" fences on account of their zigzag form. They were made of rails about 11 feet, or sometimes less, in length, and triangular in their cross-sections, each of which measured approximately from 3 to 4 inches on the base of the triangle, and from 4 to 6 inches on its sides. These rails were laid so that those of one panel of a fence crossed those of the next panel a few inches from that end of each, one rail of the one panel being laid and then one of the other until the desired height of fence was attained, the two panels forming a very wide angle; while another wide angle, the reverse of that one, was formed by the second and third panels—and so on; the panels zigzagging back and forth, in order to keep the fence from falling over. The rails were split from logs by means of an ax and a homemade maul and wedges.

When it came to sowing grain, that was done · by hand. The cutting of grain, when it was ready for harvesting, was done with a sickle. Hay was mowed with a scythe. A whetstone to sharpen sickle or scythe was frequently carried in a holder made of an ox-horn. Rakes and pitchforks were made entirely of wood. Threshing was done with a flail, or by having the grain trod by a horse or an ox.

An orchard, particularly of apple and of peach trees, was early planted on almost every farm. The apples raised were used for making apple butter, cider, and cider vinegar. Besides, both apples and peaches were cut into pieces—the apples after being pared—and dried in the sun, to be afterward used in various ways in cooking. The dried apples, as well as the pieces of apples before they were dried, were called "schnitz."

After the Germans once got live stock, they took good care of it. This meant the early

WINTER SCENE ON CONESTOGA CREEK, SOUTH OF LANCASTER

"SNAKE" OR "WORM" FENCES

building of stables, which were at first small and perhaps of a temporary character, but which in general had log walls and were covered with hay, straw, or cornstalks. Observant travelers were much impressed with the care that the Germans took of their horses and their cattle, while most other pioneers were wont to let theirs run in the woods or go without proper shelter and care in winter, in consequence of which, if their animals lived through the cold weather, they were in poor condition in the spring.

For many years there were no roads that reached to the German settlements. Such traveling as it was necessary to do was done either on foot or on horseback, along winding trails or footpaths through the woods. On horseback also grain was taken in bags to mill, and produce, with sometimes a live sheep or a live calf, was taken in panniers to the Philadelphia market. Merchandise of any kind was brought home in the same manner. Much of the marketing, moreover, was done by the women, when the distance was not too great. For service on the farms, sleds were sometimes made; and then two-wheeled carts. The wheels of the carts were solid, thick, and often of very large diameter. They were made either of cross-sections of large logs, or of pieces of wood fastened together. The carts were generally drawn by yokes of oxen; and, as the carts could stand going anywhere that there was a possibility of getting through, they came to be considerably used for transportation off the farm, as well as used on it, and helped to broaden the footpaths through the country into roadways.

In general, the German farmers hired few helpers. They preferred to do the most of their work themselves, with the assistance of the members of their immediate families, which at certain seasons of the year included the aid in the fields of their wives and their daughters. Yet they did some exchanging of work with their neighbors; and, when they did hire either men or women for service, they usually treated those hired the same as if they were regular inmates of their homes.

The most of the clothing was homemade, of homemade cloth. Sometimes boots and shoes were also homemade, but more often they were made by shoemakers who periodically went around to the houses to do the work, or to get the measurements for it. Both boots and shoes were coarse and heavy. However, men and women commonly went barefoot through the summer; and the children, a longer time. The men wore long trousers, vests, and coats or jackets, which were generally made of coarse cloth manufactured from tow and possibly dyed a brown with a preparation made from the bark of butternut trees. But trousers and jackets were frequently made of leather, or of buckskin. The women wore short gowns and petticoats. Kerchiefs, small shawls, or hoods were the usual coverings for their heads. Boys were dressed very much like their fathers; girls, like their mothers.

The housewife generally made the garden and saw to the raising of a patch of flax. She also looked after the curing and the dressing of the flax; and, with the aid of her daughters, during the winter did the spinning, and perhaps the weaving, although the materials when ready for it were sometimes sent to professional weavers to be woven. The finer grades of linen were bleached on the grass, in the sun. From the tow or coarser part of the flax not only was cloth made, but also rope for various purposes, one of which was for use as part of the harness, or "gear," for horses. After the raising of sheep was begun, the women had the wool to prepare for spinning, and then to spin. Considerable "linsey-woolsey," or coarse cloth of linen and wool, was made, and much used for clothing. Other duties frequently apportioned to the women, besides those of housekeeping, were the milking of the cows and the caring for the poultry, in addition to which they had the milk to take care of and butter and cheese to make.

On a bare table, frugal, but ample, meals were spread. Soup, bread of one kind or another, meat, and some vegetables were the main articles of diet at first for the pioneers. The meat might at times be some sort of wild game. In their seasons, there were also wild berries, some of which were made into preserves and jelly. Milk was used a great deal, but butter was to a large extent taken the place of by "smearcase" or cottage cheese, by preserves and jelly, and by apple butter, when there were apples from which to make it. Little tea or coffee was used. What was called tea was generally made of herbs; and the coffee, of burnt rye, or of burnt wheat. For seats around the table either benches or stools were utilized. But, among even a very conservative people, in the course of time various changes were inevitable, some of which should be noted.

CHAPTER IV

GENERAL LIFE AND CHANGES

The life of the Pennsylvania Germans, in general, subsequent to the days of the German pioneers was but a continuation with a gradual development or improvement in some respects of the life of the pioneers. Most of the pioneers were, after a few years, living better and getting more out of life than ever before, but with few noticeable changes in their manner of life. Nor were such changes made with any frequency by their descendants.

With regard to improving their houses there was considerable done by the second, or, if not by that, then by the third, generation. The greater number of the pioneers were inclined as long as they lived to retain their homes in their log houses, when they had good ones. But those who after them became the owners of the farms began building large stone houses, and particularly in the early part of the nineteenth century were

houses of that kind built, a fairly large proportion
of which are still in use, while the log houses
have practically all disappeared. Many of the
stone houses, however, on account of the roughness
and unsightliness of the shale stones generally
used in their construction, and the frequent development of interstices in the walls have been
plastered over on the outside with ordinary plaster, cement, or a mixture of plaster and cement,
and then perhaps painted white.

A good example of one of those old stone
farmhouses was the one which took the place of
Heinrich Rosenberger's log house. By whom
that stone house was built, and when, was not
left in doubt, because, following a custom among
many of the Pennsylvania Germans, a date-stone
or tablet—one that in this case read: "Johannes
M. Schwerdle, 1809"—was placed near the apex
of one of the gables of the house. This Schwerdle,
while yet in his minority, came as a redemptioner,
in September, 1772. Upon his arrival, his passage
was paid by Heinrich Rosenberger (son of the
pioneer), after which Schwerdle repaid the said
Rosenberger with three years of service. Subse-

quently Schwerdle married one of the daughters of that Heinrich Rosenberger, junior, and later acquired, through the will of his father-in-law and by purchase, the Rosenberger farm, on which he built that stone house. Moreover, a descendant of his—who spells his name "Swartley"—"Henry Rosenberger Swartley," is the present owner and occupant of the house and of a considerable part of the farm.

The development in the building of houses, which was from small log ones to large stone or sometimes frame ones, was fully equaled by the advance from the building of small stables to large barns, or rather to combined stables and barns, the lower part being for the stabling of horses and cattle, and the upper part for the storage of grain and hay. Some of these barns were built with stone walls; others were frame structures entirely. But the most common form was to have stone walls for the stable or lower part, and all above that built of lumber, the upper or frame part extending from 5 to 8 feet beyond the stone wall on one side of the building so as to form a partial outside shelter for live stock, or

STONE HOUSE BUILT IN 1809 ON WHAT HAD BEEN THE HEINRICH
ROSENBERGER FARM

THE RITTENHOUSE HOME NEAR GERMANTOWN
Built of stone in 1707, and later covered with plaster

sometimes for vehicles. The frame portion of many of the barns was painted white, on the outside; but, of others, red; or, sometimes, yellow.

Of some significance also was the change which was made in the building of fences. This came when people had their land for the most part cleared and under cultivation. It showed both a growing scarcity of timber from which to make rails and an increasing realization that the old worm fences, of which only a very few specimens or remnants are now to be seen, occupied an unnecessary breadth of ground and furnished too many corners in which weeds could grow, as well as soon became displeasing to the eye.

The new form of fence which was adopted, and which may yet be seen almost everywhere, except where it has been superseded by wire fencing, was constructed of posts and rails. The posts were about 7 or 8 inches wide and 2 or 3 inches thick. Lengthwise through their broader surfaces they had mortises cut that were from 2 to 3 inches wide and from 5 to 7 inches long—at such places as it was desired to have the rails. Then the posts were firmly set in the ground at

intervals of about a foot less than the length of
the rails; and the rails, hewed at their ends so
that the ends of two rails could be inserted into a
mortise, were inserted, one rail from each side,
into every mortise. That made a straight and
more durable fence, of good appearance.

The roads over which the Pennsylvania-
German farmer had to travel when he went
anywhere remained, with a few exceptions, very
poor during the most of the eighteenth century.
Especially were they rough, and at some seasons
of the year exceedingly miry in places. Sometimes
a boggy spot was improved by constructing over
it a corduroy roadbed, which was done by laying
first one log across the road and then another
beside it, continuing the operation for whatever
distance was deemed necessary. A great advance in road-making had its inception in the
incorporation in 1792 of a company that constructed a turnpike or macadamized toll-road that
was completed in 1794 between Philadelphia and
Lancaster. After that a large number of hard-
surfaced toll-roads of varying lengths were built,
and a few short ones still exist.

A considerable backwardness was also long shown in the matter of building bridges. A log was occasionally placed across a small stream, to be used as a bridge by pedestrians, but for many years any other crossing of small streams had to be done by fording them. Over large streams ferries were in the course of time established here and there. The building of substantial bridges was not begun until near the close of the eighteenth century. As late as 1795 it was said that three bridges across the Schuylkill River in the vicinity of Philadelphia were floating ones that were built of logs chained together and kept in place by anchors and by fastenings to the two shores.

When the farmers got wagons, these were usually covered ones—that is, they had canvas covers stretched over arches made of hoop-poles or bent strips of wood which were attached at their ends to the sides of the wagon boxes. Some of them were what were called Conestoga wagons, which name was perhaps in some way derived from such wagons, of heavy build, being used for transportation purposes between Philadelphia and Lancaster, or between Philadelphia and

Pittsburgh, through Lancaster; or from such wagons having been made either first or principally at Lancaster, adjacent to the Conestoga Creek. The Conestoga wagons were usually drawn by from four to eight horses. The bottom of the wagon box was made concave, or with the center a few inches lower than the ends, so that in going up and down the numerous hills the load would tend to accumulate in the center instead of sliding from one end of the wagon to the other. Like these wagons in the main were the "prairie schooners" of a later day; and somewhat of a reminder of them in appearance, especially in the expanding shape of their boxes, are the lighter, two-horse wagons, without any covers, now largely used on the farms. Another form of wagon that came to be used a great deal by the Pennsylvania Germans was a light one with either a canvas or an oilcloth cover or top. It was called a market wagon, and it is still in use, but it is gradually being displaced by automobiles.

Markets where farm produce might regularly be sold, and more general annual or semiannual markets or fairs, were established very early in

Philadelphia and in Germantown; and in other important centers, when these were formed. Markets of the first kind in particular were favored by the Pennsylvania Germans, and on their account largely are still maintained in many places. In Lancaster, for example, there are markets at certain hours on four days of the week, in three different buildings and along the curb, on one side of two streets, for about four blocks. The city owns the central market-house, and from the sale or lease of the right to use the stalls in it and of the right to use the curb for stands for market purposes during the market hours for the year of 1923 derived a revenue of about thirty-eight thousand dollars. The majority of those who conduct the markets are farmers, but in the market-house especially there are stalls maintained by butchers, bakers, and other tradesmen. Almost anything ordinarily wanted in meats, vegetables, fruits, various kinds of cheese, and pastry may be bought there. Along the curb some of the most noticeable articles offered for sale are vegetables, sauerkraut, boiled beets, potato chips, apples, Florida oranges and grape-

fruit, beef, fish, sausage, "pudding" made o
boiled and seasoned scraps of pork together witł
liver and sometimes with beef, "scrapple" oı
cornmeal mush made with the juice left after
making pudding, dressed chickens, eggs, occasionally live fowls, cottage and "Dutch" cheese,
apple butter and preserves, honey, pies, doughnuts,
and cakes. Flowers are also sold, sometimes
artificial ones. Pretzels are so much in demand
that they are continuously exposed to the dust
and for sale, at a penny apiece, at a number of
stands on the main business streets.

Going to market, either to Philadelphia or
elsewhere, meant more to the farmers in early
days than merely disposing of their produce.
It gave them new incentives to improve things,
and an opportunity to purchase much that was
needed for doing it. Thus, furniture made by
cabinet-makers or in factories came to be substi-
tuted, one article after another, for that which was
roughly homemade, especially was this true of
bedsteads, dressers, and tables, as well as of
chairs to take the place of benches and stools.
Earthenware, china, and glassware were also

CURB-MARKET SCENES IN LANCASTER

purchased at different times; likewise, articles of clothing, and cloth, until finally no more homespun was made.

The Pennsylvania Germans began to use stoves as soon as they could get them, and their houses were distinguishable in many instances by having their chimneys built through the center of the roof, and not at one end of the house as was customary for a fireplace. Later, chimneys were commonly built, on the inside of the walls, at the two ends of a house. In 1684 Pastorius asked that an iron stove be sent to him from Germany, but it was many years after that before stoves can be said to have come into use.

The first stoves were each made of five iron plates—one plate for the bottom, one for the top, one for each side, and one for the front, while the back of the stove was made by the chimney, or by an old fireplace, into which a few inches of the stove were tightly fitted. There was no opening in any of the plates. Wood, for fuel, was put in from the back, through a sort of door in the chimney or fireplace. Next, came the six-plate stove, the sixth plate being used for the back of the stove, thus permitting the stove to stand away from the chimney. This stove had a door in the front plate for the insertion of fuel. After that, the ten-plate stove was invented, the additional four plates being used in the construction of an oven in the stove. Stoves of five or six plates were usually nearly square, or possibly measured about 21 inches in height, 18 inches in width, and 24 inches in length, while ten-plate stoves were somewhat longer. The plates were generally made of cast iron and had raised ornamental or allegorical designs on what were to be their outer sides. About the middle of the eighteenth century cannon or upright cylindrical heating-stoves made their appearance, and were first used principally in large rooms frequented by the public, and in churches. All burned wood.

Baking was for a long while done in ovens, which were often of considerable size, and were generally constructed of stones and mortar at a little distance from the farmhouses, and at times in connection with smokehouses, which were used in smoking and curing meat. A great many stories have been told about what, and how much, was baked in these ovens, but their use was discontinued after the introduction, in the nineteenth century, of cook-stoves and kitchen ranges, and eventually practically all the ovens were torn down. Now the baking of bread at home has been almost abandoned, baker's bread being instead bought from wagons or automobiles sent through the country every week day to supply it.

Where there were springs or brooks, springhouses were built in which to keep the milk, cream, butter, and sometimes other articles of food. These houses—ordinarily with about the capacity of a small room, although sometimes smaller or larger than that—were usually built with stone walls, which, in the course of time, were in many instances plastered or cemented over on the outside, and painted white. But the importance and use of springhouses have been greatly diminished, in fact, in many instances their use for any purpose has been discontinued, or at times they have been converted into chicken coops, owing to the present general practice of sending either to the creameries or to the milk-dealers in the cities nearly all the milk produced on the farms, while the butter needed is being more and more purchased, instead of being churned at home; as is also at times purchased—from the creameries—even skimmed milk, when that is wanted for feed for the hogs.

Carpets did not begin to find their way into the Pennsylvania-German farmhouses until late in the eighteenth century, or the beginning of the nineteenth. In Philadelphia and perhaps in the homes of some country people where conditions favored it, before carpets came into use, clean white sand was sprinkled on the floors and deftly spread with a broom so as to form spirals and other simple, pleasing patterns. But the Pennsylvania-German housewives on farms had no time for doing that sort of thing. Besides, their ideal of a floor was one scoured scrupulously clean. However, carpets and rugs, both homemade ones and such as are sold in the stores, are now to be found in abundance in most of the farmhouses.

Candles continued long to be the main dependence for artificial lighting, but were to some extent gradually replaced with lamps of a primitive kind, in which lard was generally burned. The lamps were of many different patterns, although they were alike in principle. Some of them were made of iron, a common form of these being that of a small, shallow covered, round or oval-shaped vessel, with a handle at the side, or bent upward and with an opening or groove for the insertion through it of a wick. But more of the lamps were made of tin. These were of various sizes and shapes, some of them looking much like covered tin cups, and others like miniature teapots or oil cans of larger circumference at the base than at the top. All had handles, and most of them had a spout, on the side opposite the handle, for the wick to pass through, but some had a spout or several spouts or tubes extending upward from the top, each one to hold a wick. Not one of these lamps had a chimney. All of them were smoky, emitted disagreeable odors, and gave but a comparatively poor light. After them, in the second half of the nineteenth century, came kerosene oil lamps with glass chimneys.

The lanterns for a very long time were usually round ones made of tin perforated with either small round or longish thin holes arranged in concentric circles and other ways, through which the light from a tallow candle could shine only dimly.   Another style of tallow-candle lantern that came to be used more or less was square in its basal form, and had bottom, top, removable back, and corners from top to bottom made of tin, while the front and two sides were of glass.

Near the middle of the eighteenth century apple mills and cider presses commenced to be used.   Prior to that time cider was ordinarily made by mashing apples in a strong cask, tub, or trough by stamping them with a knot or the equivalent of wood at the end of a long handle, after which the pulpy mass was put into a kind of open-work basket that was hung to the limb of a tree, while a vessel of some sort was set under the basket to catch the juice, which was pressed out by heavy stones placed on top of the mashed apples.

A form of apple mill or grinder that came to be used, instead of the pounding or stamping to reduce the apples to a pulp, consisted of two solid cylinders about 15 inches in diameter and 20 inches in length, cut from the trunk of a tree and set upright, side by side, in a stout wooden frame, one of the cylinders extending upward as a shaft to which was attached a moderately long, strong pole or sweep, to which a horse would be hitched to operate the mill by going round and round it.   A hopper received the apples and fed them to the cylinders, one of which had notches into which the other had cogs or projections to fit.

Much more ponderous were the cider presses that were employed to press the cider out of the apple pulp.   They varied somewhat in form and size, but each press had its heavy beam, which was sometimes as much as 25 feet long and 18 inches or more square.   In some of the presses this beam was at one of its ends pivoted 3 or 4 feet above the ground in a huge post set in a strong foundation, and in the middle and at the other end upheld by some kind of a support.   The apple pulp to be pressed was put into a frame of from 3 to 4 feet square placed on a tight bottom of boards or planks directly under the beam near its pivoted end, layers of straw or of cloth being placed between layers of the pulp.   Then a movable board cover, closely fitted to the inside of the frame and having a block of wood on it so arranged that the pressure of the weight of the beam would be applied to it and press it down, was put on top of the pulp, and the weight of the beam let down upon it. Very often the frame was made of a number of frames about 3 or 4 inches deep placed on top of one another. An opening at the bottom of the frame allowed the cider, when it was pressed out, to run into a vessel set to receive it. To increase the pressure, heavy stones or blocks of wood were often put on the free end of beam. After it had been lowered, in using the press, the beam was raised again by means either of a lever on a high fulcrum or of a lengthy, vertical wooden screw about 10 inches in diameter, under the free end of the beam. When the beam was raised with a lever it was held at each new height either by wooden blocks put under it or by a strong iron pin inserted into a hole made for it in an upright standard. In order to preserve the press for many years it sometimes had a roof built over it.

Cider, however, was not made altogether for use as a beverage. For many years it was very extensively made and used for making cider vinegar for the Philadelphia market. Considerable cider was also used in making apple butter, the "schnitz" or pieces of apple being boiled in it.

The daily fare changed somewhat from that of the pioneers but in the essentials remained much the same as theirs. Some of the more common dishes of later times were bread and either scalded or cold milk; cornmeal mush and milk; soup made of potatoes, or with pieces of dough or noodles; pork with sauerkraut; pork and dumplings; sausage; liverwurst or pudding; souse or pickled pigs' feet; scrapple; bread and apple butter, preserves or jelly, and smearcase or cottage cheese; apple fritters; dried-apple and other kinds of pies; cookies, and cakes of different sorts. Most of these are favorites yet, and constitute a great portion of the meals of today. Even church suppers and those given by Bible classes in Lancaster during the winter are announced in the local newspapers most frequently as being sauerkraut, baked-ham, or roast-pork suppers.

At one time bread was often placed on the table in pieces a quarter of a loaf in size, from which each person cut as much as he wanted. Something like that is still to be seen in the somewhat common practice of putting uncut pies on the table, for each person to cut and remove with his own knife a piece of such size as he may desire. If pies of several kinds are thus served it does not necessarily mean that it is expected a piece of each will be taken. Neither is it always intended that a person shall partake of all the preserves and jellies, but rather that he may have his choice, when there are several kinds on the table. The common practice has generally been for each person, even if he be a guest, to reach for, and help himself to, whatever he wishes that is on the table. In order to facilitate the doing of this, when the table is a long one, duplicate dishes of some foods are sometimes placed at the ends of the table. Nor has it always been thought necessary to furnish spoons with the dishes from which are to be taken helpings of such articles as apple butter, preserves, smearcase, sugar, and molasses, it being considered entirely proper for each person to use his own spoon, or knife, in helping himself from any of these dishes.

In his *Travels*, Isaac Weld, junior, who referred to Philadelphia as being the largest city in the Union, and to Lancaster—which then had about nine hundred houses, most of which were built either of brick or of stone—as being the largest inland town in North America, described the taverns in 1796 as being in general very indifferent ones, mainly kept by farmers, and conducted nearly the same everywhere. He said that on their arrival travelers were shown into a room common to everyone, which room was used also as a dining-room. At night the travelers must often submit to being crammed into rooms where there was scarcely sufficient space to walk between the beds. If a traveler could procure a few eggs with a little bacon, he ought to be satisfied, as it was twenty to one that a bit of fresh meat, or any salted meat except pork, could not be had. Vegetables also appeared to be very scarce. If a person got any, it was generally either turnips, or turnip tops boiled as greens.

Other chroniclers have stated that along highways used by wagoners, when all transportation was done by wagon, it was a common practice for the wagoners to carry their own bedding, of the simplest kind, which at night they laid on the floors in the barrooms of the taverns at which they stayed. Farmers frequently did the same thing, in Philadelphia, when they went there to market. But taverns patronized largely by wagoners were often found by travelers to be particularly unpleasant places at which to lodge.

Nor would a traveler fare much better than at an ordinary tavern, if he stayed overnight at some farmhouses. This is shown by a description of table customs and home life—the outgrowth of poverty and many adverse circumstances—given by Francis Baily, president of the Royal Astronomical Society, as one of his experiences in October, 1790, in what is now Franklin County. He said that about 13 miles from Chambersburg he and a companion came at nightfall to a place which they had mistakenly understood was a tavern, which was "kept by some Dutchmen," who very reluctantly consented to letting them stay overnight. Supper was eaten with the family of seven or eight persons. The table, which had no cloth on it, was placed in the middle of the room,

THE OLDEST BUILDING IN THE CITY OF LANCASTER
The "Plough" Tavern, built about 1748

A ROW OF OLD-STYLE BUILDINGS IN LANCASTER
The sixth building from the left was the "Cat" Tavern, built about 1760

and was lighted by a blazing fire in the fireplace at one end. The meal began with warmed sour milk that was placed on the table in a large bowl, from which it was eaten by all dipping their spoons in it. After that, a dish of stewed pork, accompanied with hot pickled cabbage or hot slaw, was served and devoured in a similar manner to that in which the milk had been, or else with two or three persons eating off one plate. Then a large bowl of cold milk and bread was set on the table and partaken of in the same way as was the first dish, using the spoons just taken out of the greasy pork-dish. After supper the travelers were ushered up a ladder into a place where a small hole in the wall served as a window, and where there were four or five beds, each of which consisted of nothing more than one feather bed placed on another. The candle with which they were shown to their bed was immediately taken away. In the morning, the travelers, who, having been tired, slept soundly, discovered that they had passed the night in company with the whole family, the members of which had occupied the other beds.

Of course, not everybody even in the earliest days and in the smallest log cabins ate their meals after that fashion, or had things as dirty as it was further said those people had them. Nevertheless, among Christopher Dock's *One Hundred Necessary Rules of Conduct for Children*, which was published about 1764, there were admonitions that one should avoid everything having the appearance of ravenous hunger, such as to be the first in the dish; that one should stay at his own place in the dish; and that he should not put back into the dish what he had once had on his plate. Other injunctions were not to wipe the plate either with the finger, or with the tongue; and that greasy fingers should be wiped with a cloth, not licked. A fork should be used as much as possible, instead of the fingers; and with the point of one's knife, instead of with his fingers, should salt be taken from the salt-box. Bones and other scraps should neither be thrown under the table nor put under the table cloth, but left on the edge of the plate; and pieces of bread should not be put into the pocket, but left on the table.

Men and women toiled hard, from early in the morning until late in the evening. There was, as a rule, no compulsion on either side other than that of circumstances. Nor was there any inclination to shirk; but both men and the women undertook to do all they could; and apparently, as a class, neither especially suffered ill from it.

Life had its satisfaction for them in their having their own farms, and in their working for themselves, as also in their seeing their property increase in value, and in seeing their children grow up about as they would have them.

There were also diversions. For the men there was at times hunting; and for the boys, fishing. The men, moreover, derived considerable pleasure from the frolics or bees in which they helped one another, as in harvesting and in husking corn, when they combined with their work the exchanging of gossip, feasting and drinking, and making merry generally. Something like frolics, too, were the popular and frequently held vendues or public sales, which, shorn of some of their earlier side-attractions, are still common in some localities, particularly in Lancaster County, when people for various reasons want to sell live stock, farm equipment, or household goods.

The bees for paring and cutting apples into pieces called "schnitz," either to be dried or to be made into apple butter, might be participated in by both men and women; and, like huskings, were frequently for the young people not only occasions of social enjoyment but also of love-making.

From the time that rag carpets and quilts began to be used the women had bees for sewing carpet rags, and bees for quilting, which were as much social events as they were utilitarian affairs.

Furthermore, informal visiting between relatives and between friends living in the same neighborhood has always been popular, and has been practiced a great deal—possibly more than ever, and over a wider range of territory, since automobiles have come into general use. Besides, every year has had its holidays, and perhaps festive occasions, such as weddings, which have been whole-heartedly enjoyed.

Nor must it be forgotten that for many if not for most men of earlier times the numerous taverns that were established in the villages and along the main highways furnished places of good cheer, much like clubs, in which to congregate and discuss weather, crops, politics, and general affairs of the neighborhood. As a whole, the earlier Pennsylvania Germans were far from practicing total abstinence, although according to various reports they were much more temperate in the use of intoxicants than were some of their contemporaries of other lineage.

Children were generally reared under strict discipline, and were early taught to work, yet had their play and games. So also did the young people—who, like their parents, worked hard—have, particularly in winter, their sports, parties, and games. Dancing was popular with those who did not have religious scruples against it.

Courtships were usually begun as soon as what was regarded as a marriageable age was reached, and were conducted with vigor—occasionally either in a boorish or in what would now be deemed an improper manner. But the marriage of all young folks was looked forward to as a matter of course. Mothers often started their daughters at early ages toward filling "hope chests," or each making a chestful of quilts, household linens, and garments for use after marriage. Of the marriages that followed, apparently as large a proportion were satisfactory and happy as could possibly have been the case under any circumstances.

When a married woman speaks of her husband, she almost invariably calls him, in accordance with a widely prevalent custom, "the mister." She will say, for example: "The mister is in the field." Similarly, the husband commonly refers to his wife as "the missus."

The subjects of religion and education as pertaining to the Pennsylvania Germans will be considered together, and next.

CHAPTER V

RELIGION AND EDUCATION

Religion and education were closely related in the thoughts of the Pennsylvania Germans, and for their children the two were long promoted together, either under one roof or in adjacent buildings. The general opinion was that the work of education should be left to the church, to be either conducted or supervised by the latter, for the spiritual as well as the intellectual benefit of the children.

The great majority of the German settlers were Lutherans, members of the Reformed church, and Mennonites. Most of the others were German Baptist Brethren or Dunkers, Moravians, and Schwenkfelders, with smaller numbers of some other persuasions. Many of these people were possessed of strong religious convictions which dominated their lives, while the general character of all may be said to have been religious. Yet there were in the aggregate a considerable number

of persons who apparently left their religion, or
at least their connection with the church, behind
them, for, when they found themselves in an
environment free from ecclesiastical control, they
not only failed to ally themselves with any
religious body but neglected to attend any form
of public worship. Still others, or their descendants, becoming dissatisfied with all the old religious
organizations, formed or joined new ones.

Thus did different religious conditions prevail,
often in close proximity to one another, and give
rise to some apparently contradictory conclusions.
For instance, from some statements which have
been made a person might infer that all the German
settlers were very devout; that every company
of them brought with them their pastor; and that
houses of worship were built without much delay
and in sufficient numbers to meet all needs
therefor. On the other hand, it would appear,
from some contemporaneous accounts, that there
were many persons who were utterly indifferent
to religious matters; that various bodies of church
members were long without pastors; that sometimes when the services of the only preachers

AUGUSTUS LUTHERAN CHURCH AT TRAPPE

The oldest Lutheran church in America, built of stone in 1743, and afterward covered with plaster

LUTHERAN CHURCH

Built of stone in 1767, at New Hanover

who could be had were accepted they proved to be such that it was resolved by the congregations that thereafter no one should be allowed to preach in their pulpits without first presenting satisfactory credentials; and that many young people grew up without having any religious instruction.

At first, meetings of one form or another for worship were held in private houses. Then, here and there a small log meeting-house was built. Some of the early meeting-houses had for a while only the bare ground for their floors; others had floors built of stones, or, when procurable, occasionally of brick. In a few instances, a flat stump or a cross-section of a log served for a pulpit, and partially hewed logs for seats. The windows were small and glazed with small panes of plain glass. No provision was made until quite a late date for warming the meeting-houses in winter, and few foot-stoves were used, as most of the women were as hardy as the men.

Until well along in the eighteenth century, practically everybody who went to church either went on foot, or, when the distance was too great for that, they rode on horseback. After the two-wheeled carts came into use a family might occasionally be seen riding to church, seated on bundles of straw in a cart drawn by oxen. In the summer those who walked to church often did it barefooted, carrying their shoes in their hands until they were near the meeting-house, when they would stop to put on their shoes, and after church might stop again at the same place to take off their shoes for the walk home.

Funerals were usually attended by almost everybody for miles around. Largely owing to that fact, refreshments were served. Sometimes one person with pieces of cake in a dish, and another person with some ardent drink, would wait on the people as they arrived at the house, and a full meal would be served there after the return from the cemetery; or the meal might be served at once, if the cemetery was very far away. So much was often made of these occasions that not a few persons planned years ahead to have such feasts at their funerals as might be deemed worthy of them and be remembered appreciatively by their surviving friends and neighbors. But the unseemly results which now and then followed from inordinate drinking finally led the ministers to use their influence to have the serving of liquors in connection with funerals abolished.

Schools generally came after the organization of churches, but sometimes first. Some of the early meeting-houses were used during the week for school purposes, though usually for a limited period only, after which separate log schoolhouses were built near the meeting-houses. This meant that for many years schools were not numerous and were not easily attended by more than a few pupils.

Schoolmasters, too, were for a long time as scarce as were pastors; and some of the former proved as unfit in their sphere as did some of the latter in theirs. In some instances, pastors rendered service also as schoolmasters. Again, pastors sometimes had assistants who conducted the schools. In other cases, where there were schoolmasters and no pastors, the schoolmasters sometimes read sermons on Sunday, and, in so far as they could, looked after both the religious and the educational welfare of their communities. An exceptionally zealous schoolmaster occasionally undertook to conduct two or even three schools in rotation, so as to enable as many children and youths as possible to get the rudiments of an education.

Reverend Henry Melchior Mühlenberg, while serving as the pastor of three German Lutheran churches, wrote in his diary, in January, 1743, that, since ignorance among the youths was great, and good schoolmasters were rarely to be found, he had to take this matter also into his hands, his plan being to go to the three congregations, remaining in each successively one week. He said that it did not look very promising to see youths of from seventeen to twenty years of age appear with the "A-B-C book"; yet he rejoiced in finding the desire to learn something. When some young men came to his school who wished to learn English, he felt that also afforded him an opportunity to do good; and he read with them the New Testament in English. Singing, he said, had entirely died out among the young people.

In most of the earlier schools the instruction was given in German, and either the Bible or the New Testament was the principal textbook.

There were devotional exercises which consisted of the reading of passages of Scripture, of prayer, and of the singing of hymns. In addition to this, there was also more or less religious instruction given. The general aim was to teach the pupils to read well enough to be able to read the Bible, to spell and to write passably, and to cipher to the limited extent that it might be expected to be needed for ordinary computations. That amount of education practically all parents wanted their children—at least their boys—to have, but not much more, while it was often thought that girls would get along just as well with less. This is explained largely by the fact that most parents wanted their sons to become farmers, and expected their daughters to become the wives of farmers and to do much as the girls' mothers had done, whereas more education appeared to cause dissatisfaction with farm life. When, comparatively late, the establishment of public schools was being considered or undertaken, they were strongly objected to because they would not give the particular kind of education desired, or that which was in German, and religious.

The private and parochial schools were supported by parents paying, at a low rate, for each child they sent to school. But the meager compensation of the schoolmasters was sometimes augmented, like that of the pastors, by gifts.

An interesting description of what may be considered to have been in various respects a model school in its day is contained in Christopher Dock's *School Management*, which was written in 1750. Christopher Dock was a Mennonite, who, with others of that faith, settled near Skippack Creek in what is now Montgomery County. For ten years, commencing about 1718, he taught school there. Then he farmed most of the time for ten years, after which, owing to much solicitation, he returned to teaching, which he thenceforth continued for about thirty-two years, twelve years of the time in two schools, one in Skippack Township, and the other in Salford Township, giving three days a week to each, alternately.

He was a man of kind heart and exemplary piety who loved children, even if some of those with whom he came into contact lacked in cleanliness, or, what was worse, were prone, as he said,

THE OLDEST SCHOOLHOUSE IN GERMANTOWN

A building erected by St. Michael's Lutheran Church before 1740, and restored in 1915

CLOISTER BUILDINGS AT EPHRATA

Erected by the early German Seventh Day Baptists

to use bad words, to lie, and to steal. Except for such apparent partiality as may be required to protect children of good breeding and character from being spoiled by those ill-bred or depraved, it is the duty of the schoolmaster, he declared, to be impartial—to determine nothing by favoritism or appearance; and, if its conduct is good, or it is willing to be instructed, the poor child, for teaching which not a penny may be received, must be as dear to him as the child of the rich from whom a liberal reward may be expected.

Christopher Dock believed, furthermore, in giving children rewards for merit. He said that when a child had learned its letters its father must give it a penny, and its mother must cook for it two eggs; while, when it began to read, if it had been industrious, he himself would give it a ticket on which was written: "industrious—one penny." Sometimes he made with chalk an "O" on the hand of a child, to show that it had failed in nothing. At other times the reward was a carefully written token containing a maxim, or, more likely, a verse from the Bible; or else it was a simple, painted picture of a flower or of a bird, similar to pictures which were during a century or more given by Pennsylvania-German schoolmasters to their pupils.

Severity he considered was to be used with caution and discrimination. A timid child might be more injured than benefited if punished severely either with words or with the rod. In the same way, a stupid child might be harmed by blows, while a child accustomed to them at home would not be made right by them at school, but must be made better by some other means. However, obstinate children having no hesitation in doing wrong should be sharply punished with the rod and at the same time addressed with earnest exhortation from the Word of God, to see whether the heart could be reached. Another way in which some perverse pupils might be punished, as they were here at times, was to make them sit on what was called the punishment bench, and to compel them to wear yokes around their necks as an additional sign that they were being punished.

New pupils were assigned to volunteers among the older ones, for assistance; and to make sure that wrongdoers kept their promises of amendment they were sometimes required to get the bail or undertaking of other pupils to see that what they said they would do was done.

When such of the pupils as lived near enough to the school to get there on time arrived in the morning, those of them who could read sat down, the boys on one bench, and the girls on another. They were then given a chapter in the New Testament to read. After all had come and they had been inspected to see whether they were washed and combed, a hymn or a psalm was sung, and all kneeling recited the Lord's Prayer. Then some gave their attention to writing. Recitations of the little ones and others were heard. A chapter was given to the Testament scholars to learn; words were given to be spelled; and sometimes a quotation was given to be learned by all. Those who read letters and news sat together; likewise, those who ciphered. When a lesson was assigned, the pupils studied it aloud, according to what was said to be the custom there, as well as in England; but when the time for recitation came a rap with the rod on the table or on a bench brought silence, and one after another repeated his lesson. After the children had eaten their dinners, in order to keep them from misusing the remainder of the intermission, one or two pupils would be designated to read, until school was called, from the Old Testament—something historical; or from Moses, the Prophets, Solomon, or Ecclesiastes. Everything was in German.

When the master went from one of his schools to the other, he carried letters from pupils in the one school to those in the other, the contents of the letters being a short rhyme or a quotation from the Bible, something concerning the exercises in the school or about the motto for the week, and a question to be answered with a quotation from the Scriptures.

No attempt was made to give instruction in any one form of catechism or faith, because children of different religious opinions and practice were received into the school. It was sought, however, to make all the pupils familiar with the New Testament, by having them search through it as a whole and examine the chapters, so that they might be prepared, as it was said, to collect richly the beautiful and fragrant flowers in this Garden of Paradise.

Now the elementary education of the children of Pennsylvania-German families is obtained almost entirely in the public schools, is in English, and is of the general character of that usually afforded by such schools.

Possibly as good an example as any of a public school in a rural district at present is furnished by one located some miles east of Lancaster, while the pupils who attend it are of special interest on account of their peculiarity of dress, they being from families of the Old Order Amish, who are probably today the most conservative body of Pennsylvania Germans. The schoolhouse is a modern red-brick one, with most of the windows on one side so that the lighting is practically over the left shoulders of the pupils. In the schoolroom there are modern factory-made, individual seats and desks for about forty-five pupils, whereas, in Christopher Dock's schools, unpainted, long wooden benches, perhaps with sloping boards about 5 inches wide attached to their backs to form desks for those who sat behind them, were

used. Again, in this school illustrative of conditions now, blackboards cover all the space on
the walls available for them, while Christopher
Dock used as a blackboard in teaching ciphering
a small, narrow noteboard, with longitudinal lines
on it, designed for use in teaching music. Then,
where he either drew with the pen or painted
pictures of birds and flowers, which he gave to
his pupils, here are to be seen, arranged along
the top of the blackboard, outlines of birds,
flowers, and other objects neatly cut out of colored
paper, or painted with water colors, by the
pupils. The great difference between the modern
and the old-time school is also shown in the fact
that where, in the latter, the master made and
mended goose-quill pens for his pupils, now an
efficient mechanical lead-pencil sharpener may
be seen conveniently placed for the pupils to use
it to sharpen their lead pencils, and do it better
than it could otherwise be done, while quill pens
have long been superseded by steel ones. Furthermore, on the walls of this public school there are
pictures of Washington and Lincoln, several small
American flags and mottoes such as: "Smile,"

"Be Polite," "Be Honest," "Be Truthful."
In the windows there are some potted plants.
During the fall and winter a few large ears of
corn are displayed.

A recent teacher of the school was a young
woman who wore the white head-covering of one
of the plain sects. Most likely she was a Mennonite. She opened the school at half-past eight in
the morning by reading a psalm; the recital of
the Lord's Prayer, all standing; and leading
the singing by all of a gospel hymn, such, for
example, as "Beulah Land."

In their general character, the pupils appeared
to be about the same as those attending other
schools in adjacent country districts, although
perhaps a little more reserved in the presence of
strangers, and a little less inclined to apply themselves to some of the subjects in the course of
study, such as hygiene and language.

The boys, sitting on one side of the room, all
had their jackets off, and some of them had their
vests open. Like their fathers, they had hooks
and eyes, instead of buttons, on their jackets and
vests, but buttons were conspicuous on some of

their flannel shirts, for which latter a plain, bright blue appeared to be a favorite color. Like their fathers again, they wore their hair just a little long all around, banged in front, and without any shingling or thinning down toward the edge. Some parted their hair in the middle, while others simply combed it out straight. But that some of them had a pride in the way their hair looked was shown by one youth taking from his pocket a comb and borrowing from another lad a small mirror, with the aid of which he very carefully smoothed and arranged his thick locks. The hats worn were black, with moderately broad, straight brims, and low, flat crowns, practically like the hats worn by their fathers, except smaller. Furthermore, all wore long trousers, the color of which, like that of their jackets and vests, was generally a dark gray, a dull intermixture of black and white, or with small black and white stripes.

Just as the boys of all ages were dressed like their fathers, so were the girls in the school dressed like their mothers. The dresses of the girls were all plain and fairly long, with long sleeves and ordinary, high necks. In color, about

A TYPICAL OLD PUBLIC SCHOOLHOUSE
Adjacent to Mennonite Church and Horse Sheds, at Franconia

AMISH BOYS PLAYING BALL AT INTERMISSION OF SCHOOL

half a dozen of the dresses were purple; others were black, blue, or brown. On some of them there were plenty of buttons for fastenings, but none had them for ornament alone. The nearest things to ornaments were black collars and wrist-bands on some of the purple dresses. Besides, the greater portions of the dresses were hidden under large black aprons that reached to the bottoms of the skirts. All the girls had their hair braided and fastened in tight coils to the backs of their heads. Two or three of the older girls, who had joined the church, wore white caps or Mennonite head-dresses. In going to and from the school, all wore bonnets, the most of which were plain black ones, although some of them were common sunbonnets.

In the course of time, the Lutherans and several other denominations established schools and colleges that have developed into important institutions for the promotion of higher education.

Of the Mennonites in southeastern Pennsylvania as a religious body and as a peculiarly interesting existent, comparatively little-changed class of Pennsylvania Germans, a somewhat detailed description seems warranted.

CHAPTER VI

THE MENNONITES

The Mennonites may be regarded as in most respects typical Pennsylvania Germans, but with a somewhat interesting additional distinctiveness in their religious history and characteristics. Before they came to Pennsylvania not only had their lot been the hard one common to the masses of the German people but one frequently made harder by bitter persecution for their religious beliefs and consistent practice. Most of them came from the Palatinate, but some of them came from other parts of Germany, from Holland, and from Switzerland. They were called Mennonites because they belonged to congregations which either had been organized by Menno Simons or sought in the main to follow his interpretations of the Bible and his teachings based on them.

Menno Simons was born in Friesland in 1492. He was educated for the priesthood in the Roman Catholic church and served therein for some years, becoming quite popular. But from his study of the Scriptures he came to the conclusion that the baptism of infants was unwarranted, which led him in 1536 to renounce the Romish church and priesthood. Afterward he became the spiritual leader of a little band of people who believed as he did that the baptism of infants availed nothing, and that persons baptized in their infancy must be rebaptized on a profession of their faith, when old enough to make such profession. Then he engaged in the organization of churches or congregations, where there were people who held views similar to his, or who accepted his views—in Friesland, in Holland, and in parts of Germany. He was not so much a founder of a new church or sect as he was a gatherer-together and unifier of persons whom he found here and there believing much as he did. Nor was he an immersionist, and the Mennonites generally have not been immersionists but practicers of baptism by pouring.

The doctrine perhaps second in general importance maintained by Menno Simons was that followers of the teachings of Christ could not bear any sword but that of the Spirit, which has been one of the fundamental doctrines of the Mennonites through most of their history, being expressed in their doctrine of nonresistance or defenselessness, and practiced with firmness in an almost uniform refusal to bear arms or in any manner to participate in war.

Several other doctrines based on their interpretations of passages of Scripture, and in general strongly maintained, should also be taken into account as having contributed toward giving to the Mennonites their special religious character. They must not take any oath—must "swear not at all," but let their "communication be Yea, yea; Nay, nay." They should not hold any civil office, neither should they otherwise participate in temporal government; but they may pray for their government, pay their taxes to it, and be obedient to it in everything not contrary to the law of God. Refractory members of the church must be banned and be shunned or avoided afterward by all other members. A member of the church must not marry anyone not belonging to it. The biblical ordinances commanding the

washing of feet and the saluting of the brethren
with a kiss should be observed. The garb should
be simple. All forms of ostentation and of
worldly vanities and pleasures should be avoided.

Some of these doctrines, steadfastly held by a
determined people, frequently rendered the Mennonites obnoxious both to the authorities of the
state and to those of the church or churches
favored by the state; and at times brought dire
persecution. In consequence, at different periods
many Mennonites fled from one country to
another, as, for example, at one time seeking an
asylum in Moravia; at another time, in Holland;
and then, in the Palatinate. Very often, too,
they had to hide in the mountains and to hold
their meetings with the utmost secrecy. Along
in the early part of the eighteenth century they
began coming with some frequency to make
their homes in Pennsylvania, where they were
assured of religious liberty. They made permanent settlements in Germantown, in what are
now Montgomery and Lancaster counties, and
after that in some other places in the province.
Moreover, some of the thirteen families from

Crefeld, in Germany, who arrived in the fall of 1683 and helped to found Germantown, were Mennonites, although just how many of them were is a matter of dispute.

In 1708, the Mennonites built at Germantown their first meeting-house in America. It was small, and was built of logs. In 1770 that meeting-house was replaced with a small stone one, which, with an addition built in the rear, in 1908, for Sunday-school purposes, is still in use, having been acquired by the division of the Mennonites known as the General Conference of the Mennonites of North America, and being maintained by the latter as a sort of mission. William Rittenhouse, who in 1690 built near Germantown the first mill in America for the manufacture of paper, was the first minister of the Mennonite church at Germantown.

The Mennonite church with the largest membership at the present time is the one at Franconia, in Montgomery County. It has about seven hundred and twenty-five members. The church, or meeting, was organized, and a stone meeting-house was built, about 1730. Heinrich

THE OLDEST MENNONITE CHURCH IN AMERICA
The front part was built of stone in 1770, at Germantown

THE OLDEST BUILDING IN LANCASTER COUNTY
A house built by Christian Herr in 1719—about 6 miles southeast of Lancaster. Meetings were held in it.

Rosenberger was one of the first members, and an important one. The cemetery which adjoins the present house of worship is on what was once a corner of his farm. Heinrich Funck, a man of considerable literary and general ability, was chosen for the first minister, and was afterward made a bishop. He was also one of the two men who were selected to supervise the production of an edition in German of *The Martyrs' Mirror*.

The Bloody Theatre, or Martyrs' Mirror, which was printed in the Dutch language about 1660, was a voluminous compilation, made by Thielman J. Van Bracht, of accounts of Christians who had been opposed to infant baptism and to war and who for their convictions had suffered martyrdom, from the time of Christ up to 1660. When the war between England and France occurred and there was danger of its spreading to the colonies in America, some of the leaders of the Mennonites in Pennsylvania felt that the young men of their faith ought to have this book in the language that they could read it, in order to prepare them to maintain at any cost the observance of their fundamental doctrine that Christians should not engage in war. That led to measures being taken to have the book translated into German and some thirteen hundred copies of it printed. All the work of translation, of making the paper on which to print the book, and of printing and binding the book was done at the cloister of the German Seventh Day Baptists, at Ephrata, in Lancaster County. The undertaking was completed in 1749, after a great part of three years of labor by fifteen men, and it constituted one of the few great achievements in book-publishing in America up to that date.

As most of the Mennonites who came to Pennsylvania were farmers, they built their houses of worship at such places in their communities as they thought would best suit their convenience, which places were usually at some distance from the villages and very frequently in groves. Afterward, when considerable numbers of Mennonites had come to live around and in villages and towns, churches were often built in such centers. Those built in recent years are generally of red brick, with a seating capacity of from four to six hundred; but some of the churches have twice that capacity. The churches are invariably austerely plain, in Lancaster County being hardly distinguishable in outward appearance from some tobacco warehouses. In height, the churches are either one story, or one story above a basement. They have no steeples on them, and no church bells.

On the inside of a typical Mennonite church the walls and ceiling are plastered and calcimined. There may be a simple wainscot, and plain matting either over the whole floor or in the aisles only. The windows are constructed—with panes of ordinary size—of plain glass, and are protected during the week by tight, outside wooden shutters made with panels and painted white. The pews are made of pine lumber; are generally varnished, though sometimes painted; and are without cushions. The lighting for evening meetings, when there are any, is with electricity, where that can be obtained, otherwise with kerosene-oil lamps. The heating is still frequently done with stoves, although in the newer buildings it is generally with furnaces in the basements. There are usually separate entrances, and separate vestibules—for the men and for the women—not infrequently at both ends of the building. Sometimes, however, there are entrances on one side or on both sides or at one end and on one side of the building. A porch at one end or on one side of the church is a common thing, as in the country is also a pump conveniently near, out of doors. On the walls of the vestibules and very often of the main room, even back of the pulpit, are clothes hooks on which to hang wraps—hooks on which the men hang their black hats and in winter their overcoats, in their vestibule or vestibules, or on their side of the church; and hooks on which the women hang their black bonnets and their shawls or cloaks, in their vestibule or vestibules, or on their side of the church. Overshoes and umbrellas are also left in those same places. Moreover, on the men's side, in some of the older churches, long strips of board about 3 inches wide and having on both sides wooden pegs or iron pins or hooks about 12 inches apart are suspended from the ceiling over the middle of the rows of pews, crosswise of the pews and about 4 feet above them, or else by supports they are upheld over every other pew, lengthwise of the pews; and on those pegs or hooks the men commonly hang their hats, on account of the convenience.

In the church, the men and the boys as a rule sit on one side of the center aisle, which in some cases is on the right-hand side of it; and, in others on the left-hand side; while the women and the girls occupy the other side, whichever that is. Young boys generally sit with their fathers, and young girls with their mothers. It is also noticeable that infants form a part of almost every congregation and attract little attention even when they are fretful or noisy. Sometimes their fathers hold them; or a father holds his little girl, as does one deacon while he sits in the pulpit.

The pulpit platform, which is at one end of the room, is usually between two vestibules, and is from two to five steps high above the floor of the room, which is level. The pulpit desk may be either of only ordinary size, or of 10 feet or more in length. In any event, it is very plain, and generally painted white. Back of it are either

several plain chairs, or, more frequently an
ordinary pew that in some cases may have a
cushion on it—the only cushion in the church.
This seating is for the bishop, ministers, and
deacons, although a bishop may be present only
now and then.   There is no provision for instru-
mental music of any kind, such music being
excluded because the Mennonites hold that as a
part of religious worship it has no scriptural
grounds in the New Testament dispensation.
Nor is there any choir, but congregational singing
only.

Where there is a basement in the church
building, a small room or two may be partitioned
off in it to be used for the primary class or classes
of the Sunday-school, and at other times as a
place in which to hang wraps.   The remainder of
the basement is generally simply calcimined,
but a part of it may nevertheless be furnished
with plain tables and chairs to be used for the
serving of luncheons or meals, or to be used by
persons who bring their own lunches, when there
are occasions for it, as when there are conferences
or meetings of some kind in both the forenoon

LOG MEETING-HOUSE

Built by the Mennonites, at Landisville, about 1790

CORNER OF INTERIOR OF AN OLD MENNONITE CHURCH IN MONTGOMERY
COUNTY

Observe pews, pulpit, and clothes hooks on frame over pew near the stove

and the afternoon, or in the afternoon and the evening.

When almost all who went to church did it with horses and buggies, extensive horse sheds were built of rough lumber to be used as shelters for the teams. Those sheds, sometimes sufficient to hold nearly a hundred rigs, are in use yet, but it is mainly for automobiles, which the farmers are now generally using for going to church.

Very few of the Mennonite churches have preaching services twice, or even once, every Sunday. Most of them have preaching once in every two weeks, but some of them have it only once in four weeks. However, in many of these cases the dates are so arranged that, especially by using automobiles, the members of one church can go to another, as many of them do, when there are no services in their own church. Besides, in some instances two churches are maintained, with services on alternate Sundays, by one organization and one minister or occasionally two ministers. Evening services were long opposed, but they are now held in some churches, and, like afternoon services, which are moderately common, they are sometimes maintained in alternation with morning services on the other Sundays that there are services.

A church chooses one of its own members to be its minister, virtually for life. The usual procedure is, first, to have the members vote for, or name, the person or persons of their choice for the office. When two or more persons have thus been nominated, they are required to draw lots, following the example furnished by Acts 1:15–26. For this purpose the same number of books—usually hymnbooks—as there are nominees are taken, and in one of the books there is concealed a slip of paper with some writing on it for identification, after which each nominee draws a book, and the one in whose book the slip of paper is found is the one selected to be the minister. Before the drawing takes place, the bishop for the district may sometimes, when it appears desirable, advise that some name or names be recalled. After a minister has been duly chosen, he is ordained by the bishop, in a service held therefor. Occasionally a large church may have two ministers, or possibly three, when they are thought to be needed for the work of the church and to render assistance to other churches.

The ministers are not paid any salary, but continue by farming or through some kind of business to support themselves and their families, although when they give an unusual amount of their time and labor to some special cause, say, to conducting evangelistic services or to doing missionary work, they may, if they need it, be aided financially, as also if they fall into want. Some of them are men of considerable ability, natural oratorical power, general education, and doctrinal knowledge of the Scriptures, either in the English or in the German version. Neither collegiate nor theological education has been possessed to any extent by the ministry in southeastern Pennsylvania; nor is either apparently yet generally wanted for their ministers by the churches as a whole, which appear to be well satisfied with plain men who endeavor to preach plain biblical doctrines in a plain manner. Occasionally a doctrinal sermon will begin with Adam and the fall of man, and refer to passages or events throughout both the Old and New Testaments.

Nor have there been many changes in doctrine, as is evidenced by the statement, in *The Mennonite Year-Book and Directory*, 1923 (published in Pennsylvania), of "What Mennonites Believe," accompanied with scriptural references for every point. This shows that today they believe, among other things, in the plenary and verbal inspiration of the Bible as the Word of God; that man was created pure, and by trangression fell; that there will be a bodily resurrection of the just and of the unjust; and that the final judgment will be followed by eternal rewards and punishments. It also shows that the Mennonites still believe, as they have practically always believed, that pouring is the scriptural mode of Christian baptism; that feet-washing as a religious ceremony should be observed literally; that Christian women should wear the devotional head-covering, especially during worship; that the kiss of charity should be practiced among believers; that mixed marriages between believers and unbelievers are unscriptural; that marriages with divorced persons whose former companions are living constitute adultery; that it is unscriptural for Christian people to follow worldly fashions, engage in carnal warfare, swear oaths, hold membership in secret societies, or have their lives insured; and that obstinate sinners within the church should be expelled.

The *Rules and Discipline of the Lancaster Conference*, as revised and approved on March 22–23, 1923, go more into detail, for practical application. They provide that only a bishop shall baptize, except, in case of sickness, when the services of a bishop cannot be procured, a minister may perform the ceremony.

Before the communion (which is usually held in the spring and in the fall), the church shall be examined to learn if the members are at peace, at which time it is customary to have a sermon preached from the eighteenth chapter of Matthew, the requirements of which chapter must be complied with by members who have grievances against other members. Before the communion, too, a day of fasting and prayer should be observed. The time for the ceremonial washing of feet is immediately after the communion.

Concerning matrimony, the rules are that the nuptials shall be announced in church. Only a bishop shall solemnize the marriage of members, but a minister may officiate for others. Members who engage a minister of some other denomination in preference to their own to solemnize their marriage fall under censure. Wedding marches and flower girls are not allowed when members marry. If a member marries outside of the non-conforming churches, he is barred from the communion and the council of brethren until he acknowledges that he has trangressed the evangelical discipline of the church; but he can be reinstated by a bishop. A member marrying a person who had been divorced forfeits his membership in the church as long as the former marital partner of such person lives.

If members become proud and vain, they fall under censure. Flowers are not allowed to be placed on the remains of members, and it is advised that members do not permit flowers to be put on the remains of any persons of their families.

With regard to worldly amusements, the rule laid down is that excursion parties, surprise parties, camping-out parties by unmarried members, entertainments, all public contests in games, attending circuses, movies, theaters, helping to arrange for or attending festivals, fairs, picnics, literary societies, buying and selling tickets of chance—these, as well as all other amusements of a similar character, are forbidden.

Members are not allowed to belong to any secret society, to labor unions, to the Young Men's Christian Association, to the Epworth League, or to the Christian Endeavor Society. They are also forbidden to have life or theft insurance. If any member sues at law he is put back from the council of brethren and the communion until he acknowledges that he has transgressed against the Gospel. This conference not only does not approve of members serving in any worldly office whatever, but it earnestly advises them to keep out of those offices. For members to serve as jurors in trials for murder is forbidden, but they are allowed to serve as jurors in other cases, although they are advised to avoid such service as much as possible.

The conference recommends that Sunday-schools be held; however it does not approve of

Sunday-school libraries, unless brethren authorized by it would select a library free from fiction.

The Lord's day should be well observed. It should be made a day of devotion and worship. Church service and Sunday-school should be regularly attended. Feasting and pleasure-seeking should be strictly avoided. Both old and young should be taught how to keep the day holy, and should exercise themselves constantly to show reverence for God's house and all that pertains to it.

In choosing the ministry, which it is believed is ordained by votes and the casting of lots, the counsel of the church is to be taken, and, if favorable, then votes shall be taken. The brethren who receive votes and have the qualifications of I Timothy 3:1–13 and Titus 1:6–9 shall pass through the lot. The ministry shall not be salaried.

It is a deacon's duty to distribute to the poor members of the church; to read in the meeting the text or Scripture for the minister, when requested by him to do so; to read a portion of Scripture and pray with the congregation when no minister is present in the meeting; and, when enmity arises in the church, to look after it. But to the bishop belongs the duty, with the Word and the counsel of the church, to excommunicate the disobedient.

With these rules of the Lancaster Conference may be compared the following from the *Rules and Discipline of the Franconia Conference of the Mennonite Church*, as revised in November, 1921:

Nothing new shall enter into the church unless it be confirmed by a two-thirds vote of the conference. This conference feels the necessity of urging the leaders of the church to teach the new birth, separation from the world, nonresistance, and other essentials relative to the welfare of the church; and not to speculate on unfulfilled prophecy, as, for example, on the doctrine of the millennium.

Members are admonished against forwardness, and to be subject to those who have the rule over them according to Hebrews 13:17. They are also admonished to wear the plain clothing— are required to submit themselves to the teachings of God's Word according to I Timothy 2:8-9 and I Peter 3:3-4. The sisters shall not wear hats, fashionable clothing, gold for adornment. They shall wear the plain head-covering, and use the strings for tying; not for ornament. Parents are to dress their children as becometh their faith—not follow the world, for example, in the cutting of their hair, and in the wearing of jewelry.

The brethren are not to get costly or stylish automobiles; nor to use automobiles for pleasure, knowing that they are one of the greatest sources of evil. Good judgment should be used in running them, lest "we" become a reproach to the world.— Luke 16:15.

Members are not allowed to attend fairs, excursions, picnics, surprise parties, moving-picture shows, political meetings, parks, exhibitions, horse races, baby shows, and the like. Neither are they allowed to convey people to places of amusement which they themselves are forbidden to attend. Nor are members allowed to belong to secret societies, labor unions, farmers' unions, or temperance unions, besides which they are admonished to refrain from uniting and working with such associations as those of breeders, raisers of poultry, and producers of milk. The carrying of life insurance is also forbidden.

Members are not to accept any public office. It is considered advisable to abstain from voting.

Members shall not use the bankruptcy law. They shall not sell a mortgage unless all parties interested agree thereto. If a member makes an assignment, and his debts cannot all be paid, he is to seek the peace of the creditors, if possible, in the presence of another brother, before he can take steps to come back into the church. If a member sues to recover a debt, he is required to taken another member with him and to seek the peace of the debtor, if possible, before he can take steps to be reconciled to the church.

The different congregations are admonished to hold funerals on other days than Sunday, if possible. Flowers and other decorations are to be omitted at all funerals held in the meeting-houses, and members are not to clothe their dead in black.

This conference encourages instruction in singing.

A church belonging to the Franconia Conference has posted at the entrance to the church cemetery a printed notice that "flowering and shrubbing plants or vines are not allowed to be placed on the graves or lots in this cemetery. By order of the trustees."

The Mennonite General Conference, which was held in 1898, passed a resolution stating that the sin of worldliness whether it be made manifest in the wearing of fashionable clothing; light, frivolous talking; attending places of worldly amusements; building fashionable houses and furnishing them fashionably; or following a questionable business should be frequently pointed out and reproved from the pulpit.

A report of a committee of seven (on dress), that was adopted by the General Conference in 1913, urged the brethren to wear the kind of clothing approved by the church, avoiding all things forbidden or testified against in the Scriptures; to hold aloof from worldly fashions as manifested in changing styles in the shape and texture of hats, collars, coats, and other articles of apparel; and to hold aloof especially from such things as are manifestly worn for bodily ornamentation or because they are in style. For the

MENNONITE CHURCHES

No. 1, Franconia; 2, Line Lexington; 3, Worcester or Methacton; 4, Millwood; 5, Mellinger's; 6, Strasburg. Nos. 1 and 3 are in Montgomery County; No. 2 is in Bucks County; Nos. 4, 5, 6 are in Lancaster County. No. 4 is Amish Mennonite; 5 is a typical modern brick Mennonite church; 6 is a stone church built in 1804.

sisters the recommendations were made that they should be attired as "women professing godliness," with hair combed modestly so that the devotional head-covering might be worn with decency and order; and that they should avoid all styles indicating immodesty, low-necked dresses, short sleeves, gay colors, fabrics insufficient to cover the body properly, hobble or slit skirts, and any form of bonnet that indicated that it was worn for display rather than for service.

The local conference to which the churches in Franklin County belong has mentioned, as objectionable, creased hats; long, flashy-colored neckties; small bonnets, and small prayer head-coverings.

But not all members of the church try to observe literally all the admonitions and restrictions that are formulated; and some of these are either being slowly modified from time to time, or not rigidly enforced in one locality or another. A good illustration of a changing attitude is to be seen with reference to education. For example, the principal editorial in the *Youth's Christian Companion* of August 19, 1923, a Mennonite publication in Pennsylvania, emphasizes the value of education, with the conclusion that:

There are many reasons why, when it is at all possible, at least a high school education should be gotten. But, where there is the chance, by all means get a college education; but get it in an institution where the instructors are not of the type to undermine the Word of God.

The deacons for the Mennonite churches are chosen and ordained in practically the same manner as the ministers are, and likewise for life. Most churches have one deacon each, but there are churches that have two deacons, while in some instances there is but one deacon for two churches, as where the churches are conducted conjointly.

The bishop for a district is chosen in much the same manner as a minister is chosen, and for life. As a rule, he is chosen from the ministers of the district. His ordination is by a bishop from some other district. Bishops, ministers, and deacons do not dress in any particular respect different from other men in the church who endeavor to conform to what has been sanctioned and become customary. That calls for black or nearly black suits, with vests and medium-length coats both cut high in the neck, the coats having standing military or clerical collars about three-quarters of an inch in height, but no buttons for show on the sleeves or on the back near the waist. White collars, frequently of celluloid, are attached to the shirts, commonly with the plainest of bone collar buttons, which are generally noticeable because the more conservative men do not wear neckties, although some others, especially of the younger generation, wear them, particularly in the form of small, plain black bows. The hats in general are of black felt, and just stiff enough to hold their shape, which is with flat, round-edged crowns of medium height, and with brims about $2\frac{1}{2}$ inches wide, sometimes turned up a little at the edge. Of straw hats almost any style of plain ones may be worn in the summer; and there is an increasing tendency to wear coats and vests of the ordinary pattern. But a striking illustration of general indifference to conventionalities was recently furnished when, during a preaching service on a sultry Sunday afternoon, three of the occupants of the pulpit and many of the men in the congregation took off their coats, and, not having on any vests, displayed a variety of colored negligee shirts and the general use of suspenders. Most of the men are smooth shaven.

The garb of the women, like that of the men, is conspicuously plain and follows with remarkable closeness styles that have been long established. For their dresses, the women confine themselves mainly to plain goods and to simple colors, black predominating for the older women. But dresses of purple, blue, green, brown, gray, and of other colors are to be seen. The dresses are of plain cut and make, with high necks, long sleeves, and skirts of good length. Over their shoulders the women wear capes made of the same materials as their dresses, the capes coming to more or less of points at the waist, both in front and behind. Narrow ruching is sometimes worn in the necks of the dresses. But the most striking feature of all is the headdress. White caps made of lawn and commonly called devotional coverings or prayer head-coverings, which are believed to be required by I Corinthians 11:2–16, are worn by most of the women all through the week, but by some women only when they go to church. Over them bonnets are worn outdoors—perhaps common sunbonnets around home, but black bonnets elsewhere. The women are especially admonished to avoid vain display in ornamentation, such as the wearing of jewelry and costly clothing and the "fussing" of the hair. The wearing of gold rings is sometimes particularly inveighed against, whereas the wearing of gold-framed spectacles appears to be considered all right.

The children are generally plainly and sensibly, but not distinctively, dressed. Yet little girls are sometimes seen, even in some of the churches, with their hair tied with large bows of wide, brightly colored ribbons.

Musical instruments, such as pianos and organs, are now to be found in some homes. Daily devotional exercises are maintained in some families, as family worship, but more often each individual is left to hold such devotions in private as he may think best. Again, the heads of some families audibly ask blessings at the table, although it is a more common practice to have a silent pause before the meal, or such a pause before the meal and a like pause after it, for each person for himself silently to ask a blessing and return thanks.

What, with some variations, may be considered the present regular order of church services is the singing of a hymn; the reading of a portion of Scripture, sometimes with comments thereon; silent prayer, with all persons kneeling at the seats on which they have been sitting; the singing of another hymn; a sermon of possibly three-quarters of an hour in duration; a few words added, while remaining seated, by each of the other occupants of the pulpit than the preacher; prayer by the preacher, which he closes with the recital, by him alone, of the Lord's Prayer—all kneeling during the prayer, the singing of a hymn, announcements, and the benediction. However, the announcements may come after the benediction.

When a church is filled, on one side with men and boys, and on the other side with women and girls, all plainly clothed and apparently attentive to the service, the women with their bonnets off and their heads all alike covered with their fresh white caps, and the girls, who are not yet members of the church, with their hats removed, the devotional spirit seems to be intensified.

There is no renting of pews, and there are no ushers. Nor are collections taken at every service, but only from time to time to cover church expenses, or for special purposes. However, there are nearly always boxes that have above them the words: "The Lord loveth a cheerful giver"; yet these boxes are apparently little used, except sometimes to receive such contributions as are requested. Still, at least one important church has commenced taking collections regularly, and using small envelopes for them. Another church asked its members to pay twenty-five cents for every thousand dollars that they considered themselves worth financially, the amount so raised to be used for church maintenance for 1923, and called for a like sum for the poor fund for the year.

All services are now, as a general thing, in English, although a few churches may quite regularly have a part of their services in German, and occasionally a service entirely in German, it sometimes depending much on the language with which the preacher is the more familiar. The hymnal most frequently used is composed chiefly of selections from the common devotional hymns in English, with the addition, in a supplement at the back of the book, of a few old favorites in German. By the side of this hymnal, however, there may still be seen in some of the churches copies of *Die kleine geistliche Harfe*, which has gone through many editions, and long been used by the Mennonites.

An example of a combined German and English service with a somewhat unusual feature for these times was furnished not long ago by a service that was begun by the congregation singing an English hymn, after which a German hymn was lined in the old way, that is, one line or sentence at a time was read from the pulpit and then immediately sung by the congregation. Following that, another German hymn was sung without lining. A chapter was read from the German Bible. The congregation knelt in silent prayer. An elderly minister (from another place) preached for about half an hour in German. A younger minister followed with a fifteen-minute sermon in English. Each of the other occupants of the pulpit added a few words, either in German or in English, remaining seated while doing so. Next there was a prayer, in German, and after it the singing of a hymn, in English. Then came the benediction, in English, and after it the announcements were made in German. That was at Franconia, where the German language is still being used considerably in the meetings.

The communion is celebrated after a sermon appropriate to the occasion has been preached, generally by the bishop. In some churches in Lancaster County the men in one pew after another rise and go to the place where the bishop has taken his stand in front of the pulpit, each man in passing before the bishop receiving from him a bit of bread broken from a long slice, after which the man returns to his pew. The women then go through the same procedure. Afterward the men, and, following them the women, receive the wine in a silver cup, as they pass again before the bishop. Through a portion of the service the bishop recounts the significance of this memorial and the command to observe it, and during the remainder of the service the congregation sings appropriate hymns. In other churches the bishop passes the elements to the members, who remain in their seats, but who arise one by one to receive the bread and the wine. Participation in the communion is, as a rule, restricted to the members of each individual congregation.

On some Sunday preceding that of the communion there may be baptisms by the bishop, after a sermon usually somewhat doctrinal has been preached. Those who are to be baptized kneel in front of the pulpit, facing it; the men and the boys on one side, and the women and the girls on the other, even when there are married couples among them. The women and the girls wear the devotional head-coverings or white caps, which one of the women of the church removes, before the baptismal water is poured, and replaces after the deacon has poured a little water three times through, or between, the hands of the bishop while they are placed on the candidate's head and while the bishop speaks the words of baptism. The baptism is preceded by the bishop asking several test questions, and is followed with a prayer offered by him. The ceremony is concluded by his extending his hand to each one baptized and bidding him or her to arise to a newness of life; and when a man or a boy has risen, kissing him. The women and the girls are kissed by one or two women members of the church.

All kissing that is done under the scriptural mandate is done between men and men, or between women and women, and never between men and women. Moreover, except between officials of the church, kissing does not appear to be practiced much at the present time among the men; and, when kissing is done, it is generally done by touching the lips to the cheek adjacent to the corner of the mouth.

The washing of feet after the communion service is also solemnly and decorously performed. In some instances a number of small tubs with water in them are brought into the church and placed between the pulpit and the front row of pews, each tub between two chairs. Those who are to participate in the ceremony quietly slip off their shoes and stockings before leaving their pews, and then go forward in small numbers, the women to the tubs on their side of the church, and the men to those on their side, and seat themselves in the chairs so that there are two women at each tub on their side of the church, and two men at each tub on the men's side. Then one member of each pair at a tub washes the feet of the other, and wipes them with a towel, after which the one thus ministered to reciprocates it with a similar service. When this has been done, they arise, kiss each other, and return to their pews, whence some may go to their vestibules to put on their shoes and stockings. As the seats at the tubs are vacated, other members go forward to occupy them, which is continued until all have had a chance to follow in this way the example and what is regarded as being an enduring command of the Master. However, this ordinance is not observed at the present time in all the churches.

The Mennonites were somewhat slow about starting Sunday-schools; but now almost every church has a good Sunday-school, with a comparatively large attendance of all ages from the very young to the quite old. They are conducted in English, but some of them have classes in German for adults. They do not have festivals, picnics, excursions, rally days, nor anything of that sort. The schools are often held every Sunday, even when preaching services are not. Some churches have also young people's meetings, and occasionally conferences for the study of the Bible. Besides, considerable interest is being taken in missionary work at home and abroad, and in the establishment and maintenance of benevolent institutions.

While the church polity has always been strongly congregational, there has at the same time been a general disposition to conform to the decisions of the proper conferences, and the regular conferences now maintained furnish agencies through which the churches may co-operate in conducting missionary and charitable enterprises, as well as foster denominational institutions for higher education and provide publishing houses for the production of needed literature—things for which there is a growing appreciation. However, the inherent spirit of religious independence and congregationalism go far toward explaining why, notwithstanding that the Mennonites are naturally conservative and have maintained their fundamental doctrines with comparatively few changes, there have still sometimes been differences in views and practices in different localities, and why there have been some schisms.

The first great schism was brought about by Jacob Ammann, or Amen, who, in Switzerland near the close of the seventeenth century, urged the enforcement, through rigid discipline, of a stricter observance of the ban and avoidance, and of the washing of feet, than was commonly being practiced. Adherents to his views are called "Amish." Some of them began settling in Lancaster County in the second decade of the eighteenth century. They are now popularly divided into two classes; one of which is called the "Old Order Amish"; and the other, "Amish Mennonites," or "Progressive Amish." Sometimes the Old Order Amish are called "House

FARM BUILDINGS OF AN AMISH MENNONITE IN LANCASTER
COUNTY

AN OLD SPRINGHOUSE IN MONTGOMERY COUNTY

Amish," because they do not build churches, but have their preaching services, which are still either in German or in Pennsylvania German, first in the house of one member, and then in that of another, a dinner for all being furnished by the family at whose house the meeting is held. The Amish Mennonites, on the other hand, build churches, and have Sunday-schools (which the Old Order Amish do not have), and are occasionally designated "Church Amish." Their church services are largely in English, but sometimes wholly, or partly, in German.

As a class, the Amish confine themselves to farming, and are very successful therein. The Old Order Amish are particularly conservative—in their dress; in the furnishing of their houses, which is very plain, without carpets and without curtains; and in adopting new things which might show too much of a worldly spirit, such as automobiles and having telephones in their houses. The men wear a sort of jacket, rather than a coat, and because they have hooks and eyes, instead of buttons, to fasten their jackets and their vests, they are at times referred to as "hook-and-eye people," or as "hookers." Buttons, however, may frequently be seen on their shirts, sweaters, and overcoats, which last are generally made with capes. Another peculiarity of the men is that, while they shave their upper lips, or shave around their mouths and sometimes a considerable portion of their cheeks, yet, for the purpose of conforming to Leviticus 19:27, 21:5, they wear either short or medium-length beards and what is known as blocked, instead of shingled, hair. The Amish women dress much like other Mennonite women, except that the Amish women generally wear black shoulder-capes, whatever may be the color of their dresses, and also generally wear large black aprons.

Among the Progressive Amish, some of the men wear beards and garb of the same style as the Old Order Amish, while others are smooth shaven and wear the common style of clothes. Many of them, too, have automobiles and telephones. The women dress about as Mennonite women generally do, while the girls of all ages wear white caps or head-coverings in Sunday-school and church.

Much like the early Amish in regarding the Mennonites generally as not strict enough in the maintenance of some of their articles of faith, and perhaps today more strict in enforcing the observance of those articles than are the Old Order Amish, are the Reformed Mennonites, who were organized in Lancaster County in 1821, and are sometimes called "Herrites," or, at other times, "New Mennonites."

Other schisms have for various reasons occurred at one time or another, as, for instance, because there were men who wanted to pursue a more progressive policy of some form or other than the rest would permit, or because there were some Mennonites who had come to believe that baptism should be by immersion.

In order to distinguish from all others those who are properly called simply Mennonites, the latter are now frequently termed "Old Mennonites." Their number at the present time in the United States and Canada is given as 36,667, whereas the total number in the United States of what are classed as Mennonite bodies is placed at 91,603.

From the subjects of both religion and education the attention may be profitably turned to a consideration of the nature of the proverbs and superstition of the Pennsylvania Germans, as being somewhat indicative of the frame of mind and credulity of past generations especially.

CHAPTER VII

PROVERBS AND SUPERSTITIONS

Proverbs have been defined as being old and common sayings. These are not all embodiments of universal truths and wisdom, but are often only expressions of general opinions, and frequently of general superstitious beliefs. They have their origin in keen observations, in common experiences, and in erroneous deductions, which are finally crystallized into pithy phrasing. In all their forms they are worthy of study as somewhat illustrative of the mental development and the dominant principles of the people making or using them.

Many of the proverbs of the Pennsylvania Germans, both of those fundamentally true and of those expressive of superstitions, were brought from the fatherland, and vary somewhat in different localities, due to the fact that these were settled by people from different places. Some of the proverbs were originally in German, while others were in one dialect or another, but nearly all of them were finally given a Pennsylvania-German wording. A few of them were rather coarse.

One proverb particularly characteristic of the people may be translated: "Don't hurry; work steadily." Another describes idleness as the devil's resting-place. A third says: "Work faithfully; laziness is worse than a pestilence." There are other proverbs just as graphic and equally practical:

Morning hours hold gold.

The man who feeds his cows well churns much butter.

Earning and saving together produce the surest wealth.

A diligent housewife is the best savings-box.

One gets nothing without some trouble.

The middle course is the best way.

As one makes; so has he.

If one can get over the dog, he can get over the tail.

Who will not hear, must feel.

A rough block requires a rough wedge.

Size alone is not enough, else a cow could catch a rabbit.

He who would support himself by hunting and fishing must wear torn clothes.

Too little or too much spoils all enjoyment.

When the mice are glutted, the meal is bitter.

A person should stretch himself according to his cover.

He who does not come in time must take what is left.

Everyone must carry his own hides to the tanner.

What one does not keep in his head, he must make up for with his feet.

He who digs a pit for another will himself fall into it.

One must live, and let live.

It is better to do a little than to do nothing.

Where there is smoke there is also fire.

When a dog is hit, it yelps.

A blind hog sometimes finds an acorn.

A man who can build a good fire will make a good husband.

A woman who cuts thick slices of bread will make a good stepmother.

Who halts not, wins.

But such proverbs as the foregoing are greatly exceeded in number by those which express beliefs savoring of superstition. The latter cover a wide range of subjects, touching human life and its activities at many points, from birth to death. Some examples will sufficiently indicate the scope and character of all.

A child born on Sunday will develop pride. One born on the thirteenth of the month will have no luck. One born in the zodiacal sign of the Lion will grow up strong. One born in the sign of the Fishes will be a drinker, or always thirsty.

For a person to step over a child that is lying down will retard its growth, as will also measuring the child.

Whatever one dreams the first time that he sleeps in a place will come true.

Bubbles on a cup of coffee denote money.

If the palm of the hand itches it will soon receive money.

A person who wears round holes in the soles of his shoes will become rich, while one who wears holes in the seat of his trousers will be poor.

If one gets out of bed backward things will go wrong for him all day.

For one to forget what he was going to say is a sign that it was not true.

When a person's left ear burns it indicates that some-one is speaking ill of him, but when his right ear burns it signifies that someone is speaking well of him.

When two persons are walking together, anyone who walks between them will take away their luck.

For the cat to wash herself, or for the dog to roll on the floor is a sign that visitors will come.

If one goes into a house, he should sit down, else he will take away its peace.

Good luck is taken from a house when a stranger enters it by one door and leaves it by another.

After a person has once started from a place it is unlucky for him to return to it on account of his having forgotten something.

When the youngest in a family gets married those who are not married must either ride on the bake-oven or dance in a pig's trough. To insure good luck, one who gets married must jump over a broomstick.

In order to learn anything easily from a book, one should put the book under his pillow when he goes to bed.

Picking up a pin, or falling uphill, either one brings good luck.

To prevent a quarrel after salt has been spilled, some of the salt should be burned.

A person should never make a present of a pin, of a knife, or of a pair of scissors; nor hand to another person anything of that sort with its point toward the person to whom handed, lest it injure or sever friendship.

Some of these superstitious beliefs were not only at one time or another current everywhere among the Pennsylvania Germans, but are similar to old sayings of other people. On the other hand, some omens meant one thing to the Pennsylvania Germans in one locality, and either the opposite or a different thing to those of another community. Thus some people would say that to dream of a funeral portended a wedding, while it was more generally believed to be a sign of rain or of high water. Again, some declared that when a person's nose itched it was a sign that he would receive a letter, whereas others insisted that it was a sign of an impending quarrel. By some people the finding of a five-leaved clover was believed to bring good luck, but by others it was regarded as the forerunner of bad luck. There was a similar contradiction as to the effect of meeting a black cat. At least half-a-dozen different ills, according to beliefs held in different localities, would befall anyone who, while he had it on, let a garment be in any way sewed or mended by another person, as that the latter would sew the wearer's good luck away, would sew in the wearer's thoughts, would sew on trouble, would sew in a pain with each stitch, or the wearer would acquire an enemy, or somebody would lie about him. Similarly, there were several different beliefs as to why the back of a man's shirt should not be ironed, as that to iron it would make him lazy, or irritable, or would cause boils.

In planning and in doing his work, the farmer took into account the phases of the moon and the signs of the zodiac as he found the latter in the almanac opposite the days of the month. He was also heedful of many things expressed in proverbs concerning the weather. He said that when wild geese fly high, the weather will be warm; when low, cold. When corn husks are thick, the following winter will be a hard one; but when the corn grows beyond the husks, the winter will be mild. A hot summer portends a cold winter. In proportion to the height at which the spiders build their webs in August will be the depth of snow the coming winter. A dry April and a wet May are favorable for a large crop of hay. When the horns of the moon point downward there will be rain. Likewise, when the sun draws water, that is, when the sun's rays are visible in the clouds; when corns ache; when a cat or a dog eats grass; and when roosters sit on a fence—rain must be expected. If the sun sets under a cloud on Wednesday, rain will follow before Sunday. A ring around the moon betokens rain or snow. If chickens run for shelter when it commences to rain, the rain will not last long; but, if they run around in the rain, there will be more rain.

It was also prevalently believed that everything planted in the Lion, or sign of Leo, would grow well. Flowers should be planted in the sign of the Virgin, or, as it was sometimes said, in the sign of the Posey Woman. Potatoes should be planted during the increase of the moon, and in the sign of the Lion. Climbers, such as beans and peas, should be planted when the horns of the moon pointed upward; and not when the moon was waning. Nothing should be sowed in the Waterman, or sign of Aquarius, or it would be watery. Fruit trees would bear better after being wished a "Happy New Year." Beets would be stringy if harvested under the wrong sign, and sauerkraut made at the wrong time would be bitter.

Of course, people now do not have the faith in such things that was once manifested, nevertheless there are yet many persons, particularly among the older folks, who believe in at least some of them. As an illustration of this fact, a reporter for a Lancaster paper found that in the northern part of the county most of the stores were closed on Ascension Thursday, 1923. The reason was apparently superstition, for, two days' later, or

on May 12, the paper said editorially that while
the city pays little attention to the day, in a
business way at least, the county abides by the
older traditions. How many farmers would put
up a fence post on that day? How many of
their wives would take a needle in their hands to
sew on a missing button?   All of us still cherish
some superstition. The city man who is amused
at his country cousin's fear of lightning striking
the fence post is usually the one who knocks on
wood three times to ward off bad luck. Similarly,
the woman who has no scruples about sewing on
Ascension Day will, perhaps, after she has spilled
salt, throw some over her left shoulder; or, she
will insist on picking up every pin that she sees
on the floor or on the sidewalk.

For comparison with these old beliefs, especially
with those of them which attribute to the moon
great influence on the weather, on vegetation,
and on living beings, and for such further light
as it may throw on the subject under consideration,
the gist of a portion of an article given prominence
in a family almanac for 1923 published in Pennsylvania may be noted. That article, after

stating that Saturn was called the ruling planet for the year, said that generally the year under that planet was wet, cold, and disagreeable, although sometimes it might be very dry. Grass and vegetables were likely to start slow, and mature late. One need not be in any great haste with planting and sowing. Wheat, barley, and rye might yield good crops, but much depended on getting them cut and stored without their spoiling. The crop of hay might also be good, but it would be difficult to get it well cured. Fruit as a crop would be largely a failure, owing to the cold and inclement nature of the weather in the spring. Hops would be good, but not very plentiful. This would be a year for snakes and toads to multiply. Mice would be numerous, while worms would be fewer this year than in other years, as extreme cold weather destroys them. This year was also apt to produce much sickness toward the end of summer and during the fall—sickness taking numerous forms that are often dangerous, such as fever, diarrhea, bloody flux, catarrh, apoplexy, gout, and consumption.

With reference to the treatment of diseases and personal injuries there were in the past numerous superstitions, some of which were very crude and occasionally involved the employment of incantations. Goose oil was considered good for almost every ailment. Red beat leaves were accounted a specific for inflammation. Rheumatism was to be cured or warded off by carrying a horse chestnut in the pocket, by the wearing of an iron ring, or by tying a dried eelskin around the affected joint. For a sore throat the left stocking was to be wrapped around the neck. For nosebleed there were several remedies: to tie a red string around the neck; to tie a woolen string around the little finger; to tie an eelskin around the arm; to chew a piece of newspaper; to drop a key or a penny down the back; to pick up a stone, drop on it three drops of blood, and replace the stone just as it was, or for the person afflicted to recall who last sat next to him in church. For a toothache, one should pick the tooth with a splinter from a tree struck by lightning. Weak eyes should be washed with water from March snow. To remove freckles, they should be washed with water from an old stump.   Warts might be removed in a number of ways, one of which was to rub them with pieces of potato and bury the latter under the eaves of the house.   If a person cut himself with an ax he should cover it with grease and put it under his bed.   If he stepped on a nail he should dip it in fat and keep it in a dry place.   Hair should be cut when the moon is increasing, but corns when it is decreasing.

Following this, some side lights gathered from old records pertaining to a few individuals should be found not only of interest in themselves, but of value for what they show of more or less applicability to the Pennsylvania Germans in general, of approximately a century or a century and a half ago.

CHAPTER VIII

GLEANINGS FROM OLD RECORDS

English has been the official language of Pennsylvania from the earliest provincial times. However, neither that fact nor the consequent one that the public records of Pennsylvania have always been kept in English could ever have been counted a serious disadvantage to the Pennsylvania Germans, even when they could not read or speak English. This was so because there were usually enough persons in the various public offices who understood and spoke Pennsylvania German to make it easy for people to transact business at those offices in that language. Besides, ordinary laymen must always depend on persons technically familiar with public records to find in them what is wanted and to give to what is found its right interpretation.

But what is of more general interest now about those old records is that some of them throw light otherwise unobtainable on the Pennsylvania

Germans and their times. This is particularly true of the records of wills and estates; and some of the records of the wills and of the estates of a few members of the Rosenberger family who lived in what are now Montgomery and Bucks counties perhaps may as profitably be considered here as any of the same dates.

Heinrich Rosenberger apparently did not make any will, but, on January 19, 1745, for a stated consideration of £200, conveyed his farm of 159 acres to his son Heinrich. The making of that conveyance is the last thing actually known about Heinrich Rosenberger, the pioneer, and it may fairly be presumed it was near the close of his life, although there have been some assumptions that he lived many years beyond 1745. Those assumptions and some others concerning him may possibly be explained by a confusion of identity due to his son having the same name—Heinrich Rosenberger—and in time attracting some attention as a Mennonite minister at Franconia.

That Heinrich Rosenberger, senior, had any other child than his son Heinrich is not shown by any public record. Still it has been assumed that he had four sons: Heinrich Rosenberger; Daniel Rosenberger, who in 1740 purchased land for a farm in Hatfield Township; John Rosenberger, who about 1749 or 1750 bought land in that township; and Benjamin Rosenberger, who in 1739 settled in the township. Where these last three settled was about 6 miles southeast of Heinrich Rosenberger's farm, in another township. When or where any one of them was born is not now known. Nor is the name of any one of them to be found in the records kept of arrivals at the port of Philadelphia after 1727. That they may have been nephews of Heinrich Rosenberger, if they were not his sons, appears possible, as mere conjecture. That Daniel and John were brothers is the best attested point of relationship. All were Mennonites.

Daniel Rosenberger must have been a thrifty farmer, for to the 159 acres of land which he purchased in 1740 he was able to add 200 acres in 1769. He made his will on August 15, 1771, and died prior to September 23, 1771, since on the latter date the will was probated in the register's office in Philadelphia, as what is now

Montgomery County was a part of Philadelphia County until in 1784. The will was written in German, although the wills of the Pennsylvania Germans were generally prepared by men who could understand directions given in Pennsylvania German and write from them wills in English. Because this will was in German, there was filed. with it a translation in English, which, it was affirmed, was a true one "from the original Dutch."

The provisions which Daniel Rosenberger made in his will for his wife now appear quaint, but they were not of an exceptional character. He said, as it was translated:

I give to my loving wife Fronica [perhaps originally "Veronica," but spelled "Fronica" because pronounced much like that], for her own, our bedding and bedstead, with what is belonging to it, her chest with all the linen cloth, our pewter ware, two pots, and one cow. Likewise I give to my loving wife for her yearly maintenance, the new stove room, kitchen and cellar, what she has use for, firewood to the house, 8 bushels of rye, 5 bushels of wheat, 3 bushels of buckwheat, a fat hog of one hundred weight, apples as much as she useth, all which to be yearly during the time she remains my widow. I also give to my

loving wife two hundred pounds money for her maintenance, to use as much as she hath need of, while she
remains my widow, and the remainder to come to my
heirs.

Then, in order to make an equitable distribu-
tion among his four children—David, Isaac, Ann,
and Mary—of the remainder of his estate, and
to have his sons get the land, he made the provisions for his wife a charge against 200 acres of
land on a part of which were the farm buildings,
and devised that land to his son David, upon
whom he specifically enjoined the duty of carrying
out those provisions and of feeding and pasturing
like his own his mother's cow, in addition to which
he provided that David should pay £800 in instalments for the land, less an allowance of £100 for
time that David had been with his father.   The
remaining 159 acres of land were devised to Isaac,
who was to pay £700 in instalments for it.   The
total amount derived for the land and from all
other sources was, after the payment of all debts
and charges against the estate, to be divided
equally among the four children; but to make
it easier for David and Isaac, the share of each was

to be computed and deducted from what he was required to pay for his land.

The inventory that was filed on October 9, 1771, of the personal property left by Daniel Rosenberger placed a valuation of £14 9s. on his wearing apparel; and one of £2 2s. 6d. on his books. Significantly, too, it listed razors and a hone. Of cash, there was a little over £28; and in bonds, bills, and book accounts over £561.

Some of the articles which the widow took under the will were appraised as follows: Her chest and what was in it, £21 16s. 3d.; her bed with its furniture, £9 10s.; all the pewter, £3 4s. 3d.; a teakettle, 16s.; 2 iron pots and 1 "lead" (a large pot or caldron such as was originally made of lead), 14s.; a cow, £6. By the consent of all the children, the widow also received articles not mentioned in the will to the value of £18 16s.

Among other household goods inventoried there were a clock and case, which were appraised at £7 10s.; and a pipe stove, which was valued at £4. There were also 2 tables, 13 chairs, delftware, earthenware, tinware, knives and forks, glasses, a plain chest, a chest with drawers, a dresser, 2 large clothespresses, several beds, or bedsteads and bedding ("one bedstead and bedding in the old house"), bed-cases, sheets, pillows, pillow-cases, table cloths, hand towels, several lots of woolen cloth, blue linings, woolen yarn, linen tape, thread, hemp, tow, flax, and wool. Of household utensils there were pot racks, fire tongs, iron pots, a copper kettle, a bake-plate and "lazy bag," pans, ladles, funnels, sieves, candlesticks, a steelyard, a coffee-mill, and a conch shell which had probably been made into a dinner-horn. One big wheel and two little wheels, for spinning, were also mentioned.

For provisions there were wheat, corn, rye, barley, buckwheat, beef, pork, honey, molasses, salt, dried apples, cabbages, cheese, butter, lard, and vinegar. For domestic use there were also hops, tallow, wax, and soap. Furthermore, consonant with the times, there was some brandy in a keg and in a stone jug or jugs.

On account of the hay that was on them, two stables were mentioned; one for horses, and another for cows. There were 4 horses, 1 colt,

9 cows, 4 heifers, 2 calves, 1 bull, 10 sheep, 4 hogs, and 16 hives of bees.

Of farm and other tools, equipment, and supplies, there were listed grubbing and other hoes, shovels and spades, axes, a broadax, maul and wedges, cleaver, pick, cross-cut saw, augers, drawing knives, planes, chisels, pincers, anvil, hammers, grindstone, sheep shears, scale and weights, chains, plows, harrows, sickles, scythes, grain cradles, whetstones, rakes, pitchforks, ladders, an apple mill, windmill, wheelbarrow, cutting-box, flax brake and hatchel, gun, lantern, wagon, horse gears, currycombs, 3 saddles, 1 sidesaddle, harness leather, dressed sheepskins, upper and sole leather for shoes, parcel of window glass, lumber, shingles, nails, riddles (coarse sieves), baskets, bags, barrels, casks, tubs, pails, bottles, oats, hempseed, flaxseed, and timothy seed.

This somewhat lengthy summary of items from this inventory is given here for the purpose of throwing such light as it may on the lives of Pennsylvania-German farmers in the year 1771, by showing what things one of the well-to-do ones then had, and leaving it to be inferred from omissions in the list what things now counted necessaries were not then enjoyed.

The tax list for Hatfield Township for the year 1789 indicated that there were between seventy and eighty families in the township, while a memorandum on the last page gave this summary: 21 single men, 6,833 acres of land, 132 horses, 292 cows, 3 gristmills, 1 sawmill, 1 tan-yard. A similar memorandum on the last page of the list of taxables in 1799 for what was then Providence Township enumerated 20,639 acres of land, 269 horses, 680 head of cattle, 10 gristmills, 6 sawmills, 1 oilmill, 4 tan-yards, 12 distilleries, and 11 slaves.

Daniel Rosenberger's son David married Ann Funk, daughter of Christian Funk and granddaughter of Bishop Heinrich Funck. Christian Funk was a broad-minded, able Mennonite minister, who apparently took a more friendly attitude toward the American Revolution than some of his brethren thought that a Mennonite should take toward war, one of his contentions being that the war taxes imposed should be paid without any consideration of the use that was to be made of them. On account of the position that he took in some such matters, he was eventually expelled from the church, after which he organized a church that was composed of Mennonites who were in sympathy with his views. The first child born to David and Ann Funk Rosenberger they named "Christian."

David Rosenberger died in 1821. The year has sometimes been stated to have been 1829, but his making his will on March 7, 1821, and its being proved on September 19, 1821, show that his death occurred between those dates in 1821. His wife, Ann Funk, had died a number of years previously, and he had afterward married for his second wife, Barbara, daughter of John Dettwiler. David Rosenberger left surviving him six children by his first wife, and four by the second. The provisions which he made in his will for his wife Barbara and for his ten children, treating the latter in effect as nearly alike as possible, were of essentially the same character as those made fifty years before by Daniel Rosenberger—for his wife and children. Nor did David Rosenberger forget the children of a deceased daughter—one by his first wife.

By his will David Rosenberger gave to his wife Barbara two beds and all that belonged to them; what were called her chest and her clothespress and their contents, the chest not to be opened, inspected, or inventoried; her kitchen dresser with all the furniture thereon and therein; a clock and case; a new walnut table; 4 chairs, 2 buckets; 2 tubs; 1 iron pot; a teakettle; a fire shovel and tongs; a big wheel; a spinning wheel, and a reel; a ten-plate stove; the choice of 2 cows, which were to be pastured for her; and yearly 10 bushels of rye, 6 bushels of wheat, 4 bushels of buckwheat, as much as she might desire for her use of apples and other fruit growing on the farm; 200 pounds of good fattened pork, and 100 pounds of beef. She was also to have, for the term of her natural life, the use of either the northeast or the southwest part of the dwelling-house, whichever she might choose, with such use as she might need of the kitchen, cellar, spring-house, and bake-oven; and was to have the use of one-third of the garden, as well as was to have one-quarter of an acre of good ground sowed annually with flax seed, and was to have a sufficiency of good firewood, ready cut and split, and delivered at her door.

Most of the personal property of David Rosenberger, according to the inventory which was filed on September 19, 1821, was similar to that which his father had possessed, and included a razor, hone, and strap, appraised at fifty cents. His live stock consisted of 4 horses, 12 cows, 3 heifers, 21 sheep, and 15 hogs. He had, besides a wagon, a wagon body and cover, a sleigh, and sleds. Other things that perhaps should be noted were a lamp, 2 lanterns, slate, armchair, rocking cradle, wool cards, cider mill, frying pans, earthen pots, dough troughs, crowbar, post chisel, gun valued at seventy-five cents, smoked meat, and a barrel with whiskey, these last two being appraised as being together worth one dollar.

David Rosenberger, like his father Daniel, lived in Hatfield Township; but Christian Rosenberger, son of David Rosenberger, settled in that part of Providence Township that about 1805 was made Lower Providence Township.

AN OLD STONE HOUSE (Now Plastered Over), PERHAPS BUILT BY
CHRISTIAN ROSENBERGER EARLY IN THE NINETEENTH CENTURY

PART OF OLD CIDER PRESS WITH BEAM 25 FEET LONG
The flowers are those of the wild carrot

Christian Rosenberger has been described as having been particularly well off for a Pennsylvania-German farmer of his day. He apparently did not make any will. The inventory which was made in November, 1824, of his personal property included these valuations: 5 horses, $225; 9 cows, $130; 15 sheep, $16; 9 pigs, $9. It also showed that he had, among many other things, 4 lots of books, valued at $8; an English Bible, valued at $2; 2 shares of stock in the Bethlehem turnpike, $10; riding chair and harness, $20; dining-table, $37\frac{1}{2}$ cents; corner cupboard, $1.25; bureau, 75 cents; desk, $5; trunk, 50 cents; 1 chaff bed, 25 cents; quilts; coverlids; bread baskets; baking plank; kraut tub; sausage stuffer, 31 cents; washing machine, 25 cents; winnowing mill, $12; apple mill and trough, $2; cider press, $3; 2 barrels of cider, $4; 5 barrels of vinegar, $5; 1 still, $8; 1 decanter, $12\frac{1}{2}$ cents; 1 barrel and whiskey, 50 cents; 40 milk pots, 80 cents; 2 churns and stand, 50 cents; 2 stoves and pipe, $8; wheelbarrow, $1.25; 2 axes, $1.50; shaving horse, 25 cents; saddler's bench, 50 cents; 2 sets of horse gears, $3; sleigh,

$8; 2 harrows, $5; 37 oak posts, $2.59; 100 post
rails, $5; 1½ cords of oak wood, $3; 8 cords of
hickory wood, $24; hoop net and seine, 75 cents;
fowling piece, $1.50; clock and case, $12; one
silver watch, $1.50, and another one, $6; shaving
tools, 31 cents; and looking-glass, 12½ cents.
These valuations furnish a slight index to qualities
and values ninety-nine years ago.

A riding chair was a comparatively light, two-
wheeled, one-horse gig or carriage that began to
be seen in a few localities at a time in the eighteenth
century when most people were yet going to church
and to market on horseback.

Christian Rosenberger married an Elizabeth
Kraut, by whom he had eight children, the second
one being born in 1797, and named Jacob.

Jacob Rosenberger was a Mennonite, but in a
record of marriages solemnized by Reverend
George Wack, of the Reformed church, as published in the *Perkiomen Region, Past and Present*
(II, 115), there is this entry of 1820: "December
12. Jacob Rosenberger and Maria Dettwiler."
Jacob Rosenberger died on April 11, 1831. The
inventory of his personal property, which referred

to him as "late of Worcester Township," showed little that was different from anything that his father had; but it included, with other things: 5 horses and colts, $130; riding horse, saddle and bridle, $80; 11 cows, $178; 8 hogs, $36; 1 Dearborn wagon, cover, and gears $8; 1 market wagon and cover, $25; 1 apple mill, $5; 1 apple press, $8; plow, $1.50; 2 milk cupboards; skimmer; dripping pan; crane and pot rack, $1; andirons, 40 cents; boring machine and augers, $1.50; post spade, 75 cents; half-bushel measure, 25 cents; apple butter, $4.20; 6 barrels of vinegar, $12; 6 swarms of bees, $15; gun, 31 cents; 2 lots of books, $2.62½. No liquor was listed.

To Jacob Rosenberger and his wife eight children were born, seven of whom lived to comparatively old age, and one of whom was Jesse Rosenberger, who was born on May 1, 1827.

Jesse Rosenberger soon after he became of age set out for what was then known as the "West," and settled for a while in Stark County, Ohio, probably at Alliance, in order to follow his trade as a shoemaker, although he afterward became a farmer and a nurseryman. On June 2, 1850, he married Esther Heim, whose home was then a few miles from Alliance—in Columbiana County, Ohio—but who was born in Cumberland County, Pennsylvania, on July 16, 1833. Both of them early joined the Baptist church, and he at one time did some preaching. She died at Maiden Rock, Wisconsin, on December 12, 1871. He subsequently married again. He died at Iola, Kansas, on March 20, 1909.

The parents of Esther Heim were Leonhard Heim (as he signed his name, in German) and his first wife—whose maiden name was Mary Snyder —whom he married about 1831 in Pennsylvania, whence in 1840 they moved to Ohio. Mrs. Heim died some time prior to 1847. Mr. Heim's death is recorded in the West Township Cemetery —formerly often called the "Heim Cemetery"— at Moultrie, in Columbiana County, Ohio, on a tombstone which bears the inscription: "Leonard Heim, Died May 7, 1853, Aged 44 ys. 2 ms. 16 ds." Leonhard or Leonard Heim (by some persons spelled "Hime") learned the trade of blacksmith, but after his marriage he became a farmer. He was a member of the Lutheran church. His father was Matthias Heim, who was a farmer but at one time taught a German school. The father of Matthias Heim was, according to biographical histories pertaining to Northumberland and Schuylkill counties, Georg Heim, a man of more than ordinary intelligence and education, who, with two brothers, came from Württemberg, Germany, comparatively early in the eighteenth century. He rendered service as a schoolmaster and as a surveyor, as well as farmed. It has been quite reliably said that both Georg Heim and his son Matthias lived in Northumberland County, while there is other and strong evidence of their having lived, possibly at a little later date, in a part of Berks County that was in 1811 used in the formation of Schuylkill County. From either Schuylkill County or Northumberland County Leonhard Heim went, with two or three of his brothers, to Franklin County, after which he appears to have crossed over into Cumberland County, whence he went to Ohio, whither also went his brothers, Philipp, Johannes, and Daniel. Other brothers of his were named Georg, Samuel, Joseph, Benjamin, and, perhaps, Amos.

The westward going of Jesse Rosenberger and the settlements and removals mentioned of members of the Heim family were but examples of what many Pennsylvania Germans were doing at about that time, in order to secure such advantages as the newer sections of the country offered them.

A son born to Jesse Rosenberger and his wife, Esther Heim Rosenberger, on January 6, 1860, at Lake City, Minnesota, they named Jesse Leonard Rosenberger.

Of Jesse Rosenberger; of Jesse Leonard Rosenberger; and of Susan Esther Colver, who was born in South Abington (now Whitman), Massachusetts, on November 15, 1859, was of Puritan and Mayflower descent, was known as having been an unusually competent and successful principal of schools in Chicago, Illinois, and who became the wife of Jesse Leonard Rosenberger, and died, in Chicago, on November 19, 1918, quite full accounts have been given in *Through Three Centuries; Colver and Rosenberger Lives and Times,*

1620–1922 (Jesse Leonard Rosenberger.   Chicago: The University of Chicago Press, 1922).

In the spelling of the family names of the Pennsylvania Germans there has been a surprisingly large number of changes made for a people as much disposed as they have been to maintain their own language and identity.   There may be several reasons for this—a desire to simplify the spelling of their names, or to shorten them; an inclination to make them a little more American; or the influence exerted by school teachers, lawyers, public officials, and business men in writing or pronouncing the names in an Americanized form.

For answering the question as to what was the original spelling of a name where, as is frequently the case, there are no trustworthy old private papers or records to refer to, the public records may often be very helpful, and lead to a fairly reliable conclusion.   Such informal records as old tax lists, however, are not of much value for this purpose, since those for a number of years may have the name differently spelled almost every year, and correctly only occasionally.   Much better evidence is furnished by the signatures to deeds and to wills, or, secondarily, the records, of them.

Thus, the deed, wills, and probate records which have been cited, involving the names of Heinrich, Daniel, David, and Christian Rosenberger show quite conclusively that "Rosenberger" was the family name of each one of them.

Jacob, son of Christian, was married under the name of "Rosenberger," but at some time thereafter he changed his name to "Jacob Rosenberry," and some of his children continued to use the name "Rosenberry," while his son Jesse retained the name of "Rosenberger"—Jesse Rosenberger.

Important information about names and dates of birth and death is also frequently supplied by tombstones. For example, there are seven or eight Mennonite cemeteries in Montgomery and Bucks counties in which a number of Rosenbergers have been buried, and in most cases the name on the tombstones is spelled "Rosenberger," while the few variations in spelling the name are of such a nature as a whole as not to detract from the belief that "Rosenberger" is the original and what may be termed the proper spelling of the name. A small number of the inscriptions are in German.

But while it is supposed that Heinrich Rosenberger was buried in the Mennonite cemetery at Franconia, and that Daniel Rosenberger and his son David were buried in the cemetery of the Mennonite church at Line Lexington, in Bucks County, across the county line from where they lived in Hatfield Township, there are no tombstones to show it or to tell anything else about them. The early graves in both of those cemeteries were either unmarked or marked simply with rough pieces of common stone— generally red shale—on a few of which at one time or another names, or more frequently only initials, and sometimes dates, were scratched, as it might have been done, with a nail.

Christian Rosenberger, it has been stated, was born about 1773, and died in 1821. Both of those dates, however, are evidently erroneous, for in the Mennonite cemetery of what is called the Worcester or Methacton congregation, about a mile north of what is known as Fairview Village, there is a tombstone that was erected, as the somewhat weather-worn inscription says: "In memory of Christian Rosenberger, who departed this life November 5th, 1824, in the 53rd year of his age."

His son Jacob was buried in this same cemetery, as is shown by a tombstone inscribed: "In memory of Jacob Rosenberry, who departed this life April 11th, 1831, aged 33 years, 6 months & 22 days." Yet, as bearing on the spelling of the family name, it is significant that another tombstone, by the side of that one, reads: "In memory of Susanah Rosenberger, daughter of Jacob & Mary Rosenberger, who departed this life May 29th, 1835, aged 13 years, 4 months & 23 days."

A few tombstones erected within the last thirty or forty years for Rosenbergers buried in Mennonite cemeteries have underneath the regular inscriptions scriptural references which are designated "texts." Thus, one reads: "Text: St. Mark 13 c. 33 v." Several others respectively refer, in a similar manner, to "Isa. 57:1"; "Rev. 2:10 and Phil. 1:21"; "Ps. 132:14"; "II Tim. 4:7-8"; and "Job 29:2-5." Those over whose graves these admonitions and declarations of experience appear had attained ages ranging from fifty-six to eighty-two years, and it would seem probable that they had selected their texts.

The pious, somewhat stereotyped expressions which were frequently embodied in the introductory part of wills are well illustrated in a will that was made by a Rosenberger, in Bucks County, in 1817. This will began:

In the name of God, Amen. I . . . . (yeoman) do find myself of perfect health of body and of sound mind, memory, and understanding; thanks be given unto God. Calling unto mind the mortality of my body, and knowing that it is appointed for all men once to die, therefore I do make and ordain this my last will and testament. First of all, I recommend my soul to the hand of God Almighty, and my body I recommend to the earth, to be buried in decent Christian burial at the discretion of my executors, nothing doubting but at the general resurrection I shall receive the same again by the mighty power of God. And as touching my worldly estate wherewith it hath pleased God to bless me in this life, I give, etc.

In this last connection it may also be of some interest to note that, after the testator had made various provisions for his wife, and for the letting during her lifetime of such portions of the farmhouse and land as were not reserved for her use, he said quaintly: "And if my wife should have any inclination to keep a hog, it shall have liberty to go where the tenant's his Hogs doth go."

Another will, made in the same year by a Rosenberger in Montgomery County, began with practically the same wording as the will in Bucks County, except that this testator stated that he found himself "very weak in body, but of perfect mind, memory, and understanding—thanks be given unto God," and that this testator recommended his body to the earth "in the hope of a joyful resurrection by the merits of our Savior Jesus Christ."

In disposing of the worldly estate wherewith, as he declared, it had pleased God to bless him in this life, after enumerating a number of things which he said he gave to his "dearly beloved wife," one of those things being "my pipe stove with all that belongs to it," he added: "This all I give to my wife during her lifetime (except the pipe stove). If my wife should intermarry again, then it is my will that said stove shall devolve to my children."

A further provision of this will was: "I give to my son my Martyr Book."

These bequests not only appear somewhat strange now but indicate a valuation of a "pipe stove" and of a "Martyr Book," with a general state of mind a hundred years ago very different from any obtaining at the present time.   It would be very difficult now to find among the most conservative of the Pennsylvania-German Mennonites one who would wish to incorporate any such provisions in his will; and it would be still more difficult to find a son who would particularly appreciate the bequest of a "Martyr Book," otherwise than possibly as a cherished heirloom or memento of the past.

Likewise most of the other provisions that have been quoted from wills a century or more old and the inclusion in the inventories of brandy and whiskey clearly show different economic and other conditions and frame of mind from those which are current now.   Even the older people who cling most tenaciously to the customs, teachings, language, and associations of their early days are more or less—although it may be unconsciously—

affected by modernism operating directly or in-
directly on them through the pulpit, the Sunday-
schools, the public schools, the public press, the
daily rural delivery of mails, the wide use of
automobiles, the extensive railroad and trolley
systems, the installation of telephones, and the
things which they see and hear whenever they go
into any city or village, for no community can
be found that does not have a considerable modern
American atmosphere.

There is a strong and an increasing tendency,
moreover, among the younger people of virtually
all classes to conform as nearly as, with broadening
views, they think they rightly may, to the opinions
and ways of the world, and to enjoy all that, by
their new standards, they may be able to of its
pleasures, comforts, and luxuries, which adds to
the historic interest and importance of these
records of bygone generations, customs, and
thought.

INDEX

INDEX

American flags in school, 82

Amish, 81, 83–85, 122–25; pictures, opp. 24, 84

Ammann, or Amen, Jacob, 122

Amsterdam, 18

Amusements, worldly prohibited by Mennonites, 89, 102–3, 104, 106, 108. *See also* Diversions

Animals, domestic, 32–33, 35–38, 71–72, 145–46, 147, 150, 151, 153; wild, 4

Apple butter, 36, 41, 59, 60, 153

Apple mills and cider presses, 56–58, 146, 150, 151, 153; illus., opp. 150

Ascension Day, 134, 135

Atlantic, crossing, 17, 18–21

Automobiles, 48, 66, 97, 106, 123, 124, 164

Baily, Francis, 62

Bake-ovens, 52–53, 149

Barns and stables, 2, 37, 44–45, 145; in views, opp. 36, 44, 122

Bees or "frolics," 28, 33, 65, 66

Berks County, 10, 155

Birds, 4

Books, 19, 23, 64, 74–76, 91–92, 103–4, 131, 144, 151, 153

Boots and shoes, 38–39, 72, 146

Bridges, 47; view, opp. 10

Bucks County, 10, 140, 158, 159, 161. *See also* Mennonite churches, view of, opp. 108

Canada, 125

Carpets, 54, 66, 93, 123

"Caves," 25–27

Cemeteries, 72, 91, 107–8, 158–60

Chambersburg, 62

Character of the Pennsylvania Germans, v, 3, 8, 11, 65, 67, 69, 86, 123, 127, 163–64

Charles II, 5

Chester, 6

Chicago, Ill., 156

Children, 22, 64, 65, 67, 76–85, 95, 106, 113, 115, 124

Churches, 70–74, 90, 92–96, 123; views of, opp. 70, 90, 96, 108

Cider, 36, 56, 58–59, 151

Cider presses. *See* Apple mills; view, opp. 150

Clearing of land, 33–34

Clothing, 38–40, 51, 83–85, 89, 105–13, 123–24, 144

Colver, Susan Esther, 156

Conestoga Creek, 48; view, opp. 36

Courtships, 66, 67

Cowes, Isle of Wight, 19

Crefelders, 6, 7, 26, 90

Cumberland County, 154, 155

Custom-houses on the Rhine, 18

Customs and manners, v, 12–14, 30–32, 43, 59–64, 68, 71–72, 94–95

167

PRINTED IN THE U.S.A.

www.ingramcontent.com/pod-product-compliance
Lightning Source LLC
Chambersburg PA
CBHW070909270326
41927CB00011B/2506